STATUS and HARVESTS
of
SANDHILL CRANES

MID-CONTINENT & ROCKY MOUNTAIN
POPULATIONS

2006

Division of Migratory Bird Management
U.S. Fish and Wildlife Service
Central Flyway Representative
P.O. Box 25486, DFC
Denver, Colorado 80225

Acknowledgments

This report provides population status, recruitment information, harvest trends, and other information for the Mid-Continent (MCP) and Rocky Mountain (RMP) Populations of sandhill cranes. Information was compiled with the assistance of a large number of biologists from across North America. We acknowledge the contributions of D.S. Benning, J.L. Drahota, R.C. Drewien, J.W. Solberg, P.P. Thorpe, and R.A. Walters for conducting annual aerial population surveys; R.C. Drewien for conducting RMP productivity surveys; E.M. Martin, P.I. Padding (FWS) and J-F. Gobeil, (CWS) for conducting the Federal harvest surveys for the MCP; J. Bohne for compiling harvest information collected on sandhill cranes in the Pacific Flyway; G.L. Krapu for providing preliminary results from satellite-transmittered MCP cranes; and to D.S. Benning, E.L. Boeker, D.H. Johnson, and W.L. Kendall for consultation on the analysis of data on the status of cranes. We especially want to recognize the support of the State and Provincial biologists in the Central and Pacific Flyways for the coordination of sandhill crane hunting programs and especially the distribution of crane hunting permits and assistance in the conduct of annual cooperative surveys.

This report should be cited as: Sharp, D.E., K.L. Kruse, and J.A. Dubovsky, 2006. Status and harvests of sandhill cranes: Mid-Continent and Rocky Mountain Populations. Unnumbered. Administrative Report, U.S. Fish and Wildlife Service, Denver, Colorado 9pp.

All Division of Migratory Bird Management reports are available at our home page (http://migratorybirds.fws.gov)

STATUS AND HARVESTS
OF
SANDHILL CRANES

MID-CONTINENT AND ROCKY MOUNTAIN
POPULATIONS
2006

David E. Sharp, Central Flyway Representative, Division of Migratory Bird Management, U.S. Fish and Wildlife Service, Denver, Colorado

Kammie L. Kruse, Wildlife Biologist, Division of Migratory Bird Management, U.S. Fish and Wildlife Service, Denver, Colorado

James A. Dubovsky, Assistant Migratory Game Bird Coordinator, Division of Migratory Birds and State Programs, U.S. Fish and Wildlife Service/Region 6, Denver, Colorado

Abstract: Compared to the increases that were recorded in the 1970s, annual indices to abundance of the Mid-Continent Population (MCP) of Sandhill Cranes has been relatively stable since the early 1980s. The Central Platte River Valley, Nebraska spring index for 2006, uncorrected for visibility bias, was 183,000. The photo-corrected 3-year average for 2003-05 was 422,133, which is within the established population-objective range of 349,000-472,000 cranes. All Central Flyway states, except Nebraska, allowed crane hunting in portions of their respective states during 2005-06. About 9,950 hunters participated in these seasons, which was 8% higher than the number that participated in the 2004-2005 season. Hunters harvested 18,575 MCP cranes in the U.S. portion of the Central Flyway during the 2005-06 seasons, which was 28% higher than the estimated harvest for the previous year. The retrieved harvest of MCP cranes in hunt areas for the Rocky Mountain Population (RMP) of sandhill cranes (Arizona & New Mexico), Alaska, Canada, and Mexico combined was estimated at 13,587 during 2005-06. The preliminary estimate for the North American MCP sport harvest, including crippling losses, was 36,674, which is 11% higher than the previous year's estimate of 33,182. The long-term (1982-2004) trends for the MCP indicate that harvests have been increasing at a higher rate than population growth. The fall 2005 pre-migration survey estimate for the RMP was 20,865, which was 13% higher than the previous year's estimate of 18,510. The 3-year average for 2003-05 is 19,633, which is within established population objectives of 17,000 - 21,000. Hunting seasons during 2005-06 in portions of Arizona, Idaho, Montana, New Mexico, Utah, and Wyoming, resulted in a harvest of 702 cranes, an 18% increase from the harvest of 594 the year before.

Introduction

The MCP of sandhill cranes, the largest of all North American crane populations, is comprised of about two-thirds lesser (*Grus canadensis canadensis*), one-fourth Canadian (*G. c. rowani*), and the remainder greater (*G. c. tabida*) sandhill cranes. Collectively this population was believed to number over one-half million during the decade of the 1990's (Tacha et al.1994). The breeding range extends from northwestern Minnesota northeastward into western Quebec, then northwest through Arctic Canada, Alaska, and into eastern Siberia. The MCP wintering range includes western Oklahoma, New Mexico, southeastern Arizona, Texas, and Mexico south to near Mexico City (Fig. 1). Extensive aerial spring surveys, corrected for observer visibility bias on major concentration areas, provide annual indices of abundance used to depict population trends. These surveys are conducted in late March, when birds that wintered in Mexico, Arizona, New Mexico, and Texas usually have migrated northward to spring staging areas, but before spring "break-up" conditions allow cranes to move into Canada (Benning and Johnson 1987). The MCP Cooperative Flyway Management Plan establishes regulatory thresholds for changing harvest regulations, which are based on an objective of maintaining sandhill crane abundances at 1982-2005 levels (i.e., spring index of 411,000 ± 15%). Hunters are required to obtain either a Federal crane hunting permit or register under the Harvest Information Program (HIP) to hunt MCP cranes in the U.S. The permits or HIP registration records provide the sampling frame to conduct annual harvest surveys. In Canada, the harvest survey is based on the sales of Federal Migratory Bird Hunting Permits, which are required for all crane hunters.

The RMP is comprised exclusively of greater sandhill cranes that breed in isolated, well-watered river valleys, marshes, and meadows of the U.S. portions of the Central and Pacific Flyways (Drewien and Bizeau 1974). The largest recorded nesting concentrations are located in western Montana and Wyoming, eastern Idaho, northern Utah, and northwestern Colorado. The RMP migrates through the San Luis Valley (SLV), Colorado and winters primarily in the Rio Grande Valley, New Mexico (with smaller numbers that winter in the southwestern part of that state), in southeastern Arizona, and at several (14) locations in the Northern Highlands of Mexico (Fig. 2). During 1984-96, the RMP was monitored at a spring stopover site in the SLV. However, cranes from the MCP also began to use this area, which confounded estimates of RMP abundance. In 1996, a fall pre-migration (September) survey replaced the spring count as the primary tool for monitoring population change. The RMP Cooperative Flyway Management plan established population objectives, a survey to monitor recruitment, and harvest levels that are designed to maintain a stable abundance between 17,000 - 21,000 birds (Pacific and Central Flyway Councils 1997). The plan contains a formula for calculating allowable annual harvests to achieve population objectives. All sandhill crane hunters in the range of the RMP must obtain a state permit to hunt cranes, which provides the sampling frame for independent state harvest estimates and allows for assignment of harvest quotas by state. In many areas, harvest estimates are supplemented by mandatory check-station reporting.

Mid-Continent Population of Sandhill Cranes

No sport hunting seasons for MCP cranes were allowed in the U.S. between 1916-60. In the Central Flyway, areas open to hunting were gradually expanded during 1961-74, but subsequently have remained relatively stable. Operational hunting seasons are now conducted annually in portions of Colorado, Kansas, Montana, New Mexico, North Dakota, Oklahoma, South Dakota, Texas, and Wyoming. Nebraska is the only Central Flyway state that currently does not have a crane sport hunting season. Areas open to crane hunting in the Central Flyway during 2005-06 are shown in Fig. 3.

During the 1961-74 expansions of sandhill crane hunting, hunters gradually improved knowledge of sandhill cranes and improved their hunting success. During 1975-85, a tradition of sandhill crane hunting became established. Together with improvements in the equipment (decoys, calls, clothing, blinds, etc.) and a shift from pass-shooting and hunting on roosts to decoy-hunting in fields, crane hunter success increased (Sharp and Vogel 1992). Since the mid-1980s, average seasonal bags, an indicator of hunter success, have been relatively stable.

In North Dakota, sandhill crane seasons resumed in 1968 and were incrementally expanded thereafter. During 1968-79, the number of counties open for crane hunting increased from 2 to 8. From 1980-92, the number of counties with open seasons increased to 30, and were grouped into two zones. Beginning in 1993, the zones were eliminated and Federal frameworks were fully utilized for the designated hunting area (Sharp and Cornely 1997). In 1993, Kansas became the ninth Central Flyway state to initiate a crane hunting season within established Federal frameworks. As with most other states, initial seasons in Kansas were more restrictive than Federal frameworks allowed. In 2001, designated hunt areas in North Dakota and Texas were expanded, with the new areas having reduced frameworks.

The MCP included at least 510,000 sandhill cranes in March 1982, the last extensive survey involving high-altitude vertical photography of major spring migration staging concentrations. Beginning in 1982, an intensive photo-corrected ocular-transect survey of Nebraska's Central Platte River Valley (because >95% of the MCP are generally found in this area during late March) and ocular assessments from other spring staging areas have been used to monitor the annual status and trends for this population (Table 1). The March 2006 index for the Central Platte River Valley, which has not yet been corrected for visibility bias (Table 1, Fig. 4) was 183,000 birds. This estimate was less than half of the previous year's index of 412,300. Just prior to this year's survey (March 28), a spring snowstorm dropped heavy amounts of precipitation across central Nebraska during March 18-21 (U.S Dep. of Commerce & U.S. Dep. of Agriculture. Weekly weather and crop bulletin – March 28, 2006. 93(13):1-20). Snowfall totals of 21.6 in. at Grand Island, 21.2 in. at Hastings and 16.7 in. at Kearney set one day snowfall records and blanketed crane feeding sites along the river corridor. In response, large numbers of sandhill cranes traveled long distances (> 5 miles away from roosting sites on the river) to locate accessible feeding sites. This event likely moved cranes outside the survey area, particularly to other areas in Nebraska which recorded 70,000 cranes during the survey, a 158% increase in the number reported the previous year (27,100). The annual photo-corrected estimates and 95% confidence intervals for the Central Platte River portion of the survey indicate a relatively stable (*P*=0.53) population trend for the MCP since 1982 (Fig. 5). The average index for photo-corrected counts during

3

2003-05 is 422,133 cranes, which is 16% higher than the previous 3-year average of 363,167 (Solberg 2006), and remains within the management threshold objective levels (349,000 -472,000 cranes) (Fig. 6).

Since 1975, special Federal Sandhill Crane Hunting Permits or HIP certification have been required for all crane hunters participating in seasons in the Central Flyway. A sample of these permittees are mailed questionnaires soon after the completion of each hunting season. The resulting responses enable estimation of hunting activities and success in each geographic area or state (Martin 2005).

During the 2005-06 seasons in the Central Flyway, 67,554 hunters were either HIP-certified or obtained crane hunting permits, which were not limited in number (Table 2), with 9,948 individuals hunting at least one time (Table 3). The number of active hunters was the highest recorded and is 8% higher than the previous year's estimate of 9,171 (Fig. 7). The number of hunters in Texas (53%) and North Dakota (34%) combined comprised 87% of sandhill crane hunters in the Central Flyway. Federal frameworks allowed daily bag/possession limits of 3/6, which most states selected (only portions of North Dakota and Texas had lower bag and possession limits). Specific dates selected by states in the Central Flyway for 2005-06 were similar to those of previous hunting seasons (Table 4).

Crippling-loss rates (number of cranes lost/[number of cranes lost + retrieved]) in the U.S. portion of the Central Flyway continued a long-term decline (R^2 = 0.927, P < 0.01) from over 16% in 1975 to a preliminary estimate of about 9% during the most recent hunting season (Fig. 8). The number of days afield per hunter increased to about 3.6 days per hunter, which is the second highest level recorded since surveys were initiated in 1975 (Fig. 9). The preliminary estimated seasonal bag per hunter also increased to about 1.9 birds per hunter (Fig. 10). The preliminary estimate of retrieved and unretrieved mortality associated with the sport harvest in the Central Flyway (20,370) was 28% higher than the previous year's estimate (15,870) (Fig. 11). The increasing trend (R^2 = 0.523, P < 0.01) in the Central Flyway's harvest of MCP cranes during 1975-2004 likely was related to the gradual increase in hunter opportunity combined with improved knowledge of crane behavior and hunting techniques (Sharp and Vogel 1992).

Cranes from the MCP also are harvested in the RMP hunt areas in Arizona and New Mexico, in Alaska (Table 5), and in Canada and Mexico. The estimate of the 2005-06 sport harvest in Canada (Manitoba and Saskatchewan) was 9,877, which was 11% lower than the previous year's estimate (Table 6). The preliminary harvest estimate for Alaska, and the RMP hunt areas in Arizona and New Mexico combined was 786 birds for 2005-06. For Alaska, sandhill crane harvest in harvest zones 1-6 are believed to be mostly MCP cranes and zones 7-12 are sandhill cranes from the Pacific Population of lesser sandhill cranes. There also is some intermingling of MCP cranes with RMP cranes in portions of New Mexico and Arizona; however, bag checks allow individual harvest estimates for each population. There are no annual harvest surveys in Mexico, but annual MCP harvests probably are <10% of the retrieved harvest in the U.S. and Canada (R. Drewien, personal communication). This assumed low level of harvest was supported by an independent assessment of harvest in Mexico (Kramer et al. 1995). The 2005-06 preliminary estimate of retrieved and unretrieved kill of MCP cranes by sport hunters was 36,674, 11% higher than last year's estimate of 33,182 (Table 7, Fig. 12).

To assess the relative rates of change between population size (abundance) and harvest, we used linear regression on the natural log-transformed values for these variables for the years 1982-2004. Because >10% of the MCP occurs outside the Central Platte River Valley (CPRV) in the spring of some years, we combined the photo-corrected counts in the CPRV with the ocular cruise estimates from areas outside the CPRV for analyses of population abundance. For harvest, we used only the estimates of retrieved harvest for the Central Flyway, RMP hunt areas in Arizona and New Mexico, Alaska, and Canada, because crippling-loss rates for the latter three areas are unknown and no empirical estimates of harvest from Mexico are available. Regression of the log-transformed values indicate a non-significant slope for the abundance values ($P = 0.20$; $R^2 = 0.078$; slope = + 0.7% per year change), suggesting no trend in the abundance of cranes over the time frame. However, the regression of the harvest values suggested an increase in the rate of harvest over that same time period ($P < 0.01$; $R^2 = 0.67$; slope = + 2.6% per year) (Fig. 13). These results suggest that the increase in the rate of harvest is increasing faster than the rate of growth in crane abundance.

Subsistence harvest levels of MCP sandhill cranes historically were poorly documented. However, the recent U.S./Canada Migratory Bird Treaty Amendment will result in improvements to sandhill crane harvest-monitoring programs in both the U.S. and Canada. Intensive studies conducted on the Yukon-Kuskokwim (Y-K) Delta, Alaska in 1999 reported an MCP harvest of 3,907 adults and fledged young and 920 eggs. These estimates are similar to long-term averages (1989-98) of 3,362 adults and fledged young and 547 eggs taken by subsistence hunters on the Y-K Delta. Efforts are being made to gather additional information on subsistence harvests for the remainder of Alaska, Siberia, and Canada.

Rocky Mountain Population of Greater Sandhill Cranes

The RMP was not hunted in the U.S. from 1916 until 1981, when Arizona initiated the first modern-day season. Since 1982, hunting programs have been guided by a cooperative management plan, including a harvest strategy, that has been periodically updated and endorsed by the Central and Pacific Flyways (Kruse et al. 2006). Special limited hunting seasons during 2005-06 resulted in an estimated harvest of 702 RMP sandhill cranes (Table 8), which was 18% higher than the previous year (Fig. 14).

Counts conducted in the SLV during the spring migration suggested that the number of RMP cranes was relatively stable during 1984-96 (Table 9). However, survey biologists found that these estimates contained increasing numbers of the MCP (Canadian and lesser subspecies). An adjustment, using ground-derived proportions, was made to correct for the lesser subspecies (Benning et al. 1996). Unfortunately, a similar correction could not be made for the mid-sized Canadian subspecies, and in 1996 the survey was discontinued (Fig. 15). In 1997, an attempt was made to survey these cranes during the fall (October) in the SLV, but MCP cranes also were present at that time. Biologists concluded that neither a spring nor a fall count in the SLV would result in a reliable index to the abundance of the RMP. As an alternative, a cooperative 5-state September pre-migration staging-area survey, experimentally tested in 1987 and 1992, has been ongoing operationally since 1995. It was designated as the official count for the RMP in 1997 (Table 10). Although operational in 1995 and 1996, the survey was variable in timing and survey effort. What appears to be a decrease in the population estimates (Fig. 16) in 1995 and 1996 is likely more an artifact of inconsistent survey effort. The 2005 fall survey resulted in an index of 20,865 birds (Drewien et al. 2005). The 2005 survey was determined to be reliable by survey biologists and the resulting 3-year average of 19,633 is within the established population objectives (17,000 - 21,000) (Fig. 16). Because no other known crane population co-mingles with them during that time, the September pre-migration survey for the RMP appears to be a good alternative to either a spring or fall survey in the SLV.,.

During 1986-95, important breeding areas in the Intermountain West experienced extremely dry conditions and indices of recruitment (% juveniles) were low (generally between 4-6%) (Fig. 17). A return to more favorable breeding conditions during1996-99 resulted in higher recruitment rates (8-12%), but a return to drier conditions resulted in lower production during 2000-02. There was some improvement in breeding areas in 2003-04 and recruitment rates again increased to above average levels. Biologists believe that the production outlook for the 2006 breeding season will remain above average. Based on current RMP population and recruitment indices, management guidelines allow for a maximum take of 1,321 birds during 2006-07 hunting seasons.

Discussion and Research Implications for Management of Sandhill Cranes

1. Satellite transmitters placed on sandhill cranes during spring at the Platte River, Nebraska allowed the tracking of MCP cranes as they traversed U.S. states, provinces and territories in Canada, northeastern Asia, and Mexico during 1998-2003. The study tracked 150 cranes during their annual cycle and will have far-reaching management implications, including: (1) resolving critical issues related to harvest regulations, (2) determining spatial and temporal distribution patterns of subspecies, (3) assessing annual bias of population estimates, (4) identifying breeding, migration, and wintering habitat affinities to better target habitat conservation programs, and (5) refining techniques for monitoring a wide range of species of migratory birds that spend parts of their annual cycle in remote regions of North America or Asia. Satellite tracking information is available at the following Internet address (G.L. Krapu, personal communication):
   http://www.npwrc.usgs.gov/perm/cranemov/cranemov.htm

2. A research study to estimate survival rates from leg-banded RMP cranes was completed several years ago (Drewien et al. 2000). Although this information provided insight into distributions, fidelity, and mortality factors, the sample size was inadequate to accurately estimate survival rates. A new study has been initiated to estimate survival rates from approximately 10,000 resighting observations of RMP color-marked and neck-collared cranes (Drewien et al. 2002). Further, the researchers will attempt to develop a model of recruitment for these cranes. The overall goal is to develop a model of population dynamics, which would allow improvements in the harvest strategy for this population of cranes. The revision of the cooperative management plan for the RMP is scheduled to begin during winter 2006-07.

3. North American sandhill crane biologists currently recognize three subspecies of sandhill cranes in the MCP; however, the existence of the mid-sized crane subspecies has been questioned for many years. Recent genetics research

6

suggests substantial interbreeding between the greater (*G.c. tabida*) and the mid-sized subspecies (*G.c. rowanii*)(Rhymer et al. 2001, Johnson et al. 2003, Petersen et al. 2003). Final results from genetics research and subsequent morphological investigations may allow biologists to make determinations regarding the classification of MCP into subspecies, and revisions of management plans will consider this new information.

4. The agricultural landscape, on which sandhill cranes depend for a portion of their annual cycle, has undergone dramatic changes in recent years. In particular, some areas have experienced changes in the types of crops planted, harvest efficiency has increased, and genetically modified crops are being introduced. In 2004, Regions 1, 2, and 6 of the U.S. Fish and Wildlife Service and the U.S. Geological Survey collaborated to initiate a range-wide assessment of habitats used by the RMP, and how changes in habitats influence the timing and duration of use by cranes. Additionally, ongoing and proposed research by the Northern Prairie Wildlife Research Center will investigate how reduced waste grain availability in the Platte River Valley may impact the distribution and abundance of cranes. Results of these studies will enable managers to better target habitat actions which benefit cranes.

References

Aldrich, J.W. 1979. Status of the Canadian sandhill crane. Pages 139-148 *in* J.C. Lewis, ed. Proceedings 1978 Crane Workshop. Colorado Sate University Printing Service, Ft. Collins, Colorado.

Benning, D.S. 1996. Spring Survey - Rocky Mountain Population of Greater Sandhill Cranes. Special report in the files of the Central Flyway Representative. Denver, Colorado. 6pp.

Benning, D.S., R.C. Drewien, D.H. Johnson, W.M. Brown, and E.L. Boeker. 1996. Spring population estimates of Rocky Mountain Greater Sandhill Cranes in Colorado. Proceedings North American Crane Workshop 7:165-172.

Benning, D.S., and D.H. Johnson. 1987. Recent improvements to sandhill crane surveys in Nebraska's central Platte River Valley. Proceedings North American Crane Workshop 5:10-16.

Buller, R.J. 1979. Lesser and Canadian sandhill crane populations, age structure, and harvest. U.S. Fish and Wildlife Service Special Scientific Report 221. 10pp.

Buller, R.J. 1981. Distribution of sandhill cranes wintering in Mexico. Pages 266-272 *in* J.C. Lewis, ed. Proceedings 1981 Crane Workshop. National Audubon Society, Tavernier, FL.

Central,, Mississippi and Pacific Flyway Councils. 1981, 1993, and 2006. Management Plan for the Mid-Continent Population of Sandhill Cranes. Special Report in files of the Central Flyway Representative. Denver, Colorado.

Drewien, R.C., and E.G. Bizeau. 1974. Status and distribution of greater sandhill cranes in the Rocky Mountains. Journal of Wildlife Management 38:720-742.

Drewien, R.C., W.M. Brown, and W.L. Kendall. 1995. Recruitment in Rocky Mountain Greater Sandhill Cranes and comparisons with other crane populations. Journal of Wildlife Management 59:339-356.

Drewien, R.C., W.M. Brown, and D.S. Benning. 1996. Distribution and abundance of sandhill cranes in Mexico. Journal of Wildlife Management 60:270-285.

Drewien, R.C., P.P. Thorpe, and D.S. Benning. 2005. September 2005 count of the Rocky Mountain Population of Greater Sandhill Cranes. Special Report in the files of the Pacific Flyway Representative. Portland, Oregon. 8pp.

Drewien, R.C., W.M. Brown, D.C. Lockman, W.L. Kendall, K.R. Clegg, V.K. Graham, and S.S. Manes. 2000. Band recoveries, mortality factors, and survival of Rocky Mountain greater sandhill cranes, 1969-99. Report submitted to the U.S. Fish and Wildlife Service, Division of Migratory Bird Management, Denver, CO.

Drewien, R.C., W.L.Kendall, J.A. Dubovsky, and J.H. Gammonley. 2002. Developing a survival model for Rocky Mountain Population of greater sandhill cranes. Proposal submitted to the FWS Webless Migratory Bird Program, Denver, CO.

Johnson, D.H. 1979. Modeling sandhill crane population dynamics. U.S. Fish and Wildlife Service Special Scientific Report 222. 10pp.

Johnson, D.H., J.E. Austin, and T.A. Shaffer. 2003. A fresh look at the taxonomy of Midcontinental Sandhill Cranes. Proceedings of the 2003 North American Crane Workshop. In Press.

Johnson, D.H., and W.L. Kendall. 1997. Modeling the population dynamics of Gulf Coast sandhill cranes. Proceedings of the Seventh North American Crane Workshop 7:173-179.

Johnson, D.H., and R.E. Stewart. 1973. Racial composition of migrant populations of sandhill cranes in the northern plains states. Wilson Bulletin 85:148-162.

Kendall, W.L., D.H. Johnson, and S.C. Kohn. 1997. Subspecies composition of sandhill crane harvest in North Dakota, 1968-94. Proceedings of the Seventh North American Crane Workshop 7:201-208.

Kramer G.W., E. Carrera, and D. Zavaleta. 1995. Waterfowl harvest and hunter activity in Mexico. Transactions North American Wildlife and Natural Resources Conference 60:243-50.

Kruse, K.L., D.E. Sharp and J.A Dubovsky 2006. Population status, hunting regulations, and harvests of the Rocky Mountain Population of Greater Sandhill Cranes. Proceedings of the 2006 North American Crane Workshop. In Press.

Lochman, D.C., L. Serdiuk, and R.C. Drewien. 1987. An experimental greater sandhill crane and Canada goose hunt in Wyoming. Pages 47-57 in J.C. Lewis, ed. Proceedings 1985 Crane Workshop. Platte River Whooping Crane Habitat Maintenance Trust, Grand Island, Nebraska.

Martin, E.M. 2005. Sandhill crane harvest and hunter activity in the Central Flyway during the 2004-05 hunting season. Unnumbered Administrative Report, U.S. Fish and Wildlife Service, Laurel, MD. 12pp.

Miller, H.W. 1987. Hunting in the management of mid-continent sandhill cranes. Pages 39-46 in J.C. Lewis, ed. Proceedings 1985 Crane Workshop. Platte River Whooping Crane Habitat Maintenance Trust, Grand Island, Nebraska.

Montgomery, J.B. Jr., 1997. Sandhill crane use of the Mid-Pecos Valley of New Mexico. Proceedings North American Crane Workshop 7:157-164.

Pacific Flyway Council and Central Flyway Council. 1982, 1987, 1991 and 1997. Management Plan of the Pacific and Central Flyways for the Rocky Mountain Population of Greater Sandhill Cranes. Special Report in the files of the Pacific Flyway Representative. Portland, Oregon.

Petersen, J.L., R. Bischof, G.L. Krapu, and A.L. Szalanski. 2003. Genetic variations in the midcontinental population of sandhill crane, *Grus canadensis*. Biochemical Genetics 41:1-12.

Rhymer, J.M., M.G. Fain, J.E. Austin, D.H. Johnson, and C. Krajewski. 2001. Mitochondrial phylogeography, subspecific taxonomy, and conservation genetics of sandhill cranes (*Grus canadensis*; Avers: Gruidae). Conservation Genetics 2:203-218.

Schmitt, C.G., and B. Hale. 1997. Sandhill crane hunts in the Rio Grande Valley and southwest New Mexico. Proceedings North American Crane Workshop 7:219-231.

Sharp, D.E., and J.E. Cornely. 1997. Summary of sandhill crane hunting seasons in North Dakota, 1968-94. Proceedings of the North American Crane Workshop 7:209-218.

Sharp, D.E., J.A. Dubovsky, and K.L. Kruse. 2005. Status and harvests of the Mid-Continent and Rocky Mountain Populations of sandhill cranes. Unnumbered. Administrative Report, U.S. Fish and Wildlife Service, Denver, CO. 8pp.

Sharp, D.E., and W.O. Vogel. 1992. Population status, hunting regulations, hunting activity, and harvests of the mid-continent population of sandhill cranes. Proceedings North American Crane Workshop 6:24-32.

Solberg, J.W. 2006. Coordinated spring mid-continent sandhill crane survey. Unnumbered Administrative Report, U.S. Fish and Wildlife Service, Bismarck, ND. 10pp.

Tacha, T.C., S.A. Nesbitt, and P.A. Vohs. 1994. Sandhill Cranes. Pages 77-94 *in* T.C. Tacha and C.E. Braun, eds. Migratory Shore and Upland Game Bird Management in North America. International Association of Fish and Wildlife Agencies, Washington D.C.

Tacha, T.C., and P.A. Vohs. 1984. Some population parameters of sandhill cranes from mid-continental North America. Journal of Wildlife Management 48:89-98.

Table 1. Annual spring abundance indices for the Mid-Continent Population of sandhill cranes.

	CENTRAL PLATTE RIVER VALLEY, NE				OTHER						ALL AREAS			
	OCULAR CRUISE TRANSECT	OCULAR TRANSECT	PHOTO CORRECTED OCULAR TRANSECT								OCULAR CRUISE TRANSECT	OCULAR TRANSECT	PHOTO CORRECTED OCULAR TRANSECT	
YR			ANNUAL	3-YR AVG	OTHER NE	KS	CO[1]	OK[1]	NM[1]	TX			ANNUAL	3-YR AVG
1974	162,600				9,000	1,900	0	400	0	3,200	177,100			
1975	223,600				2,300	900	500	100	100	tr	227,500			
1976	147,500				2,800	300	0	100	1,000	800	152,500			
1977	173,400				1,100	1,600	0	400	12,500	30,700	220,000			
1978	149,800	188,582			2,200	700	0	0	2,300	4,900	159,900	198,682		
1979		203,574			2,600	1,100	500	1,500	0	0		209,274		
1980	223,400	254,417			5,000	4,100	0	100	500	1,400	234,500	265,517		
1981		248,882			8,300	11,200	500	0	0	21,800		290,682		
1982		347,996	417,263		7,100	2,000	2,800	0	100	7,800		367,796	437,063	
1983		306,316	343,378		4,100	200	0	200	tr	7,000		317,816	354,878	
1984		222,710	261,802	340,814	18,100	900	0	1,100	tr	800		243,610	282,702	358,214
1985		378,127	514,763	373,314	11,500	3,000				1,200		393,827	530,463	389,348
1986		317,025	353,040	376,535	1,000	200				2,100		320,325	356,340	389,835
1987		383,581	416,058	427,954	0	tr				400		383,981	416,458	434,420
1988		386,853	463,457	410,852	0	0				7,700		394,553	471,157	414,652
1989		391,353	391,995	423,837	100	1,000				800		393,253	393,895	427,170
1990		385,950	412,154	422,535	11,000	5,200				10,300		412,450	438,654	434,569
1991		297,831	340,645	381,598	100	800				200		298,931	341,745	391,431
1992		257,709	406,457	386,419	12,200	300				1,100		271,309	420,057	400,152
1993		253,799	378,883	375,328	16,800	37,750				13,500		321,849	446,933	402,912
1994		395,543	477,215	420,852	14,600	0	2,400			0		412,543	494,215	453,735
1995		273,376	326,181	394,093	30,400	0	6,700			0		310,476	363,281	434,810
1996		318,514	519,984	441,127	7,600	0	3,900			0		330,014	531,484	462,993
1997		350,932	534,630	460,265	16,200	100				0		367,232	550,930	481,898
1998		337,203	530,848	528,487	13,600	100				0		350,903	544,548	542,321
1999		219,800	284,900	450,126	3,500	100,000				0		323,300	388,400	494,626
2000		484,600	490,100	435,283	16,900	26,100				500		528,100	533,600	488,849
2001		387,300	413,500	396,167	10,500	42,300				3,500		443,600	469,800	463,933
2002		309,000	315,000	406,200	17,100	15,100		5,800		1,200		348,200	354,200	452,533
2003		300,900	348,000	358,833	24,800	4,100				3,800		333,600	380,700	401,567
2004		365,400	426,500	363,167	17,700	1,200		100		2,200		386,600	447,700	394,200
2005		412,300	491,900	422,133	27,100	2,900		2,600		8,700		453,600	533,200	453,867
2006[2]		183,000			70,000									

[1] CO, OK, and NM were eliminated from the Official Survey Area in 1985 by the CF CMU.
[2] Preliminary

D.E. SHARP   S:\CF D\projects\CRANES.mcp\Sheramey\   06.13.06

Table 2. Federal Mid-Continent sandhill crane permits issued in the Central Flyway.

YR	CO	KS	MT	NM	ND	OK	SD	TX	WY	TOTAL
1975	401		158	1,225	4,172	171	198	5,482	56	11,863
1976	341		117	1,195	4,137	265	200	5,060	37	11,352
1977	374		82	1,452	6,294	519	134	4,897	48	13,800
1978	343		209	956	5,798	620	98	5,198	52	13,274
1979	528		159	1,288	4,949	470	63	5,098	43	12,598
1980	437		118	1,082	5,754	510	240	5,239	33	13,413
1981	397		53	1,022	5,796	466	197	5,297	30	13,258
1982	528		147	962	4,714	750	579	4,650	40	12,370
1983	575		175	706	8,033	909	528	7,317	63	18,306
1984	538		113	721	7,436	1,187	544	6,838	43	17,420
1985	555		143	710	6,802	1,102	656	7,417	59	17,444
1986	617		99	595	8,926	1,073	705	7,258	25	19,298
1987	610		128	502	8,778	1,213	517	6,289	30	18,067
1988	512		162	480	6,214	1,472	437	7,053	38	16,368
1989	434		172	430	6,128	1,717	524	8,066	25	17,496
1990	389		143	533	7,268	1,725	646	11,994	22	22,720
1991	501		238	602	3,353	1,618	668	11,142	25	18,147
1992	498		303	582	3,760	1,397	721	9,848	18	17,127
1993	411	575	336	541	4,572	1,277	708	10,407	37	18,864
1994	427	567	320	547	4,790	1,561	636	10,515	49	19,412
1995	571	711	351	564	5,242	1,323	650	10,755	42	20,209
1996	612	837	369	499	5,570	1,391	677	11,334	41	21,330
1997	572	997	325	454	4,934	1,393	757	37,365[2]	46	46,843
1998	4,937[2]	1,088	270	449	6,082	1,385	951	32,523[2]	49	47,734
1999	4,847[2]	1,235	279	516	6,050	1,438	810	33,380[2]	52	48,607
2000	5,169[2]	1,084	283	493	7,451	1,333	721	44,719[2]	58	61,311
2001	5,869[2]	1,374	253	509	8,078	1,315	680	49,410[2]	72	67,560
2002	5,644[2]	1,279	303	496	8,245[2]	1,186	619	37,558[2]	54	55,384
2003	5,854[2]	1,206	273	471	6,030[2]	1,000	563	43,199[2]	50	58,646
2004	5,784[2]	1,180	308	548	5,788[2]	780	307	52,161[2]	61	66,917
2005[1]	5,766[2]	805	281	494	7,441[2]	698	490	51,511[2]	68	67,554
AVERAGES:										
1975-79	397		145	1,223	5,070	409	139	5,147	47	12,577
1980-89	520		131	721	6,858	1,040	493	6,542	39	16,344
1990-99	1,377	859	293	529	5,162	1,451	722	17,926	38	28,099
2000-04	5,664	1,225	284	503	7,118	1,123	578	45,409	59	61,964
1975-04	1,643	1,011	213	704	6,038	1,086	524	16,582	43	27,238
CURRENT YEAR PERCENT CHANGE FROM:										
2004	0%	-32%	-9%	-10%	29%	-11%	60%	-1%	11%	1%
1975-79			94%	-60%	47%	71%	254%		44%	
1980-89			115%	-31%	8%	-33%	-1%		76%	
1990-99		-6%	-4%	-7%	44%	-52%	-32%	187%	78%	140%
2000-04	2%	-34%	-1%	-2%	5%	-38%	-15%	13%	15%	9%
1975-04		-20%	32%	-30%	23%	-36%	-7%		57%	148%

[1] Preliminary

D.E. SHARP   S:\CF D\projects\CRANES\mcp\Shcranerep.xls   06/13/06

[2] Harvest Information Program (HIP) or a point-of-sale electronic record used to identify crane hunters in lieu of a special sandhill crane hunting permit

Table 3. Estimated active Mid-Continent sandhill crane hunters[1] in the Central Flyway.

YR	CO	KS	MT	NM	ND	OK	SD	TX	WY	TOTAL
1975	226		69	806	2,896	80	117	2,733	22	6,949
1976	203		68	752	1,328	148	80	2,497	16	5,092
1977	189		40	921	4,126	339	77	2,329	27	8,048
1978	190		86	836	3,776	334	50	2,390	21	7,683
1979	275		61	745	3,225	307	29	2,356	13	7,011
1980	216		50	625	3,387	275	160	2,439	12	7,164
1981	216		23	598	3,315	269	103	2,543	14	7,081
1982	138		56	386	2,429	342	260	1,553	8	5,172
1983	211		64	253	3,551	384	225	2,435	20	7,143
1984	206		51	301	3,189	467	208	2,380	19	6,821
1985	187		37	216	2,383	372	168	2,613	12	5,988
1986	106		17	178	3,095	299	149	1,991	5	5,840
1987	113		29	133	2,529	358	120	1,942	5	5,229
1988	117		48	171	1,779	531	78	2,497	11	5,232
1989	74		52	152	2,018	492	153	2,805	6	5,752
1990	101		33	180	2,614	395	172	4,130	6	7,631
1991	153		69	220	1,674	370	139	3,231	3	5,859
1992	96		95	182	1,776	330	153	2,655	7	5,294
1993	87	294	97	218	2,223	357	140	3,602	5	7,023
1994	93	293	79	211	2,497	456	151	3,350	11	7,141
1995	154	393	118	211	2,408	331	143	3,707	6	7,471
1996	91	382	82	166	2,744	355	169	3,356	9	7,354
1997	67	452	68	124	2,386	264	178	4,515	10	8,064
1998	96	480	43	155	2,785	345	237	4,022	10	8,173
1999	133	533	60	204	2,444	375	173	2,699	8	6,629
2000	192	430	64	160	2,481	223	209	3,180	11	6,950
2001	202	555	72	173	2,934	391	145	3,554	13	8,039
2002	175	517	85	166	2,407	237	144	4,037	15	7,783
2003	236	495	60	244	2,271	64	114	4,821	10	8,315
2004	315	539	93	252	2,491	265	79	5,121	16	9,171
2005[2]	273	264	85	231	3,349	243	165	5,314	24	9,948

AVERAGES:

	CO	KS	MT	NM	ND	OK	SD	TX	WY	TOTAL
1975-79	217		65	812	3,070	242	71	2,461	20	6,957
1980-89	158		43	301	2,768	379	162	2,320	11	6,142
1990-99	107	404	74	187	2,355	358	166	3,527	8	7,064
2000-04	224	507	75	199	2,517	236	138	4,143	13	8,052
1975-04	162	447	62	331	2,639	325	144	3,049	12	6,903

CURRENT YEAR PERCENT CHANGE FROM:

	CO	KS	MT	NM	ND	OK	SD	TX	WY	TOTAL
2004	-13%	-51%	-9%	-8%	34%	-8%	109%	4%	50%	8%
1975-79	26%		31%	-72%	9%	1%	134%	116%	21%	43%
1980-89	72%		99%	-23%	21%	-36%	2%	129%	114%	62%
1990-99	155%	-35%	14%	23%	42%	-32%	0%	51%	220%	41%
2000-04	22%	-48%	14%	16%	33%	3%	19%	28%	85%	24%
1975-04	69%	-41%	36%	-30%	27%	-25%	15%	74%	105%	44%

[1] Those permittees reporting hunting cranes 1 or more times

D.E. SHARP   S:\CF_D\projects\CRANES\mcp\Shcranerep.xls   *06/13/06*

[2] Preliminary

Table 4. Season dates (month/day) for the hunting of sandhill cranes in the Central Flyway states.

YR	CO	KS	MT[1]	MT[2]	NM	ND[1]	ND[2]	OK	SD	TX[1]	TX[2]	TX[3]	WY
1960	-	-	-	-	01/01-01/30	-	-	-	-	11/04-12/03	-	-	-
1961	-	-	-	-	11/04-12/03	-	-	-	-	11/03-12/02	-	-	-
1962	-	-	-	-	11/03-12/02	-	-	-	-	11/02-12/01	-	-	-
1963	-	-	-	-	11/02-12/01	-	-	-	-	10/31-11/29	-	-	-
1964	-	-	-	-	10/31-11/29	-	-	-	-	10/30-11/28	-	-	-
1965	-	-	-	-	10/30-11/28	-	-	-	-	10/29-11/27	-	-	-
1966	-	-	-	-	10/29-11/27	-	-	-	-	11/04-01/02	-	-	-
1967	10/01-10/30	-	-	-	11/04-01/02	-	-	-	-	-	-	-	-
1968	10/01-10/30	-	-	-	11/02-12/28	11/09-12/08	-	12/14-01/02	11/09-12/08	11/02-12/28	12/14-01/02	-	-
1969	10/04-11/02	-	-	-	11/01-12/28	11/08-12/07	-	12/13-01/11	11/08-12/07	11/01-12/28	12/13-01/11	-	-
1970	10/03-11/01	-	-	-	10/31-01/10	11/14-12/13	-	12/05-01/10	11/14-12/13	10/31-01/10	12/05-01/10	-	-
1971	10/02-11/07	-	-	-	10/30-01/30	11/13-12/02	-	12/04-01/30	11/13-12/02	10/30-01/30	12/04-01/30	-	-
1972	10/01-11/05	-	10/01-11/06	-	11/03-01/31	11/11-12/10	-	12/02-01/28	11/11-12/10	10/28-01/28	12/02-01/28	-	10/07-11/05
1973	10/01-11/05	-	09/29-11/04	-	10/27-01/27	11/10-12/09	-	12/01-01/27	11/10-12/09	10/27-01/27	12/01-01/27	-	10/13-11/11
1974	10/01-11/05	-	09/28-11/03	-	10/26-01/26	11/09-12/08	-	11/30-01/26	11/09-12/08	10/26-01/26	11/30-01/26	-	10/12-11/10
1975	10/04-11/08	-	10/04-11/09	-	10/25-01/25	11/08-12/07	-	11/29-01/25	11/08-12/07	10/25-01/25	11/29-01/25	-	10/11-11/09
1976	10/02-11/06	-	10/02-11/07	-	10/30-01/30	11/06-12/05	-	11/27-01/23	11/06-12/05	10/30-01/30	12/04-01/30	-	10/09-11/07
1977	10/01-11/06	-	10/01-11/06	-	10/28-01/29	09/07-09/11	-	11/26-01/22	09/07-09/11	11/01-01/31	12/05-01/31	-	10/08-11/06
1978	09/30-11/05	-	09/30-11/05	-	10/28-01/29	09/07-09/11	-	11/25-01/21	09/07-09/11	10/31-01/31	12/05-01/31	-	10/07-11/05
1979	10/13-11/18	-	09/29-11/04	-	10/27-01/27	09/07-09/11	-	11/24-01/20	09/07-09/11	10/30-01/30	12/04-01/30	-	10/13-11/18
1980	10/11-11/16	-	10/04-11/09	-	10/30-01/31	09/06-09/14	09/06-09/10	11/22-01/18	09/20-09/28	10/31-01/31	12/05-01/31	-	10/11-11/16
1981	10/10-11/15	-	10/03-11/08	-	10/31-01/31	09/05-09/20	09/05-09/13	11/22-01/18	09/20-09/28	10/31-01/31	12/05-01/31	-	10/03-11/08
1982	10/02-11/28	-	10/02-11/28	-	10/31-01/31	09/04-09/19	09/04-09/12	10/23-01/23	10/02-11/11	10/30-01/30	12/04-01/30	-	09/25-11/21
1983	10/01-11/27	11/06-01/02	11/01-11/27	11/01-11/27	10/29-01/28	09/10-11/06	09/10-09/30	10/22-01/22	10/01-11/06	11/12-02/12	12/03-02/12	01/14-02/12	09/24-11/20
1984	09/29-11/25	11/05-01/01	09/29-11/25	11/01-11/25	10/27-01/25	09/08-11/04	09/08-09/28	10/13-01/13	09/29-11/04	11/10-02/10	12/01-02/10	01/12-02/10	09/22-11/18
1985	09/28-11/24	11/05-01/01	09/28-11/24	11/01-11/24	10/26-01/26	09/07-11/03	09/07-09/27	10/12-01/12	09/28-11/03	11/09-02/09	11/30-02/09	01/11-02/09	09/21-11/17
1986	10/04-11/30	11/02-12/29	10/04-11/30	11/01-11/30	10/25-01/25	09/06-11/02	09/06-10/03	10/11-01/11	09/28-11/02	11/08-02/08	11/29-02/08	01/03-02/08	09/20-11/16
1987	10/03-11/29	11/01-12/28	10/03-11/29	10/03-11/29	10/24-01/24	09/05-11/01	09/05-10/02	10/10-01/17	09/26-11/01	11/14-02/14	11/28-02/07	01/02-02/07	09/19-11/15
1988	10/01-11/27	11/07-01/03	10/01-11/27	10/01-11/27	10/22-01/22	09/10-11/06	09/10-09/30	10/22-01/22	09/24-10/30	11/12-02/12	11/26-02/05	01/07-02/12	09/17-11/13
1989	09/30-11/26	11/06-01/02	09/30-11/26	09/30-11/26	10/21-01/21	09/09-11/05	09/09-09/29	10/21-01/21	09/30-11/05	11/11-02/11	12/02-02/11	01/06-02/11	09/16-11/12
1990	09/29-11/25	-	09/29-11/25	09/29-11/25	10/20-01/20	09/08-11/04	09/08-10/14	10/20-01/20	09/29-11/04	11/10-02/10	12/01-02/10	01/05-02/10	09/15-11/11
1991	09/28-11/24	-	09/28-11/24	09/28-11/24	10/19-01/19	09/07-11/03	09/07-10/13	10/19-01/19	09/28-11/03	11/09-02/09	12/07-02/09	01/04-02/09	09/15-11/11
1992	10/03-11/29	-	09/26-11/22	09/26-11/22	10/17-01/17	09/05-11/01	09/05-10/11	10/17-01/17	09/26-11/01	11/14-02/14	12/05-02/14	01/02-02/07	09/15-11/11
1993	10/02-11/28	11/06-01/02	09/25-11/21	09/25-11/21	10/16-01/16	09/11-11/07	09/11-11/07	10/16-01/16	09/25-10/31	11/13-02/13	12/04-02/13	01/08-02/13	09/15-11/11
1994	10/01-11/27	11/05-01/01	09/24-11/20	09/24-11/20	10/15-01/15	09/10-11/06	09/10-11/06	10/15-01/15	09/24-10/30	11/12-02/12	12/03-02/12	01/07-02/12	09/14-11/10
1995	09/30-11/26	09/30-01/01	09/23-11/19	09/23-11/19	10/31-01/31	09/09-11/05	09/09-11/05	10/22-01/28	09/23-11/19	11/11-02/11	12/02-02/11	01/06-02/11	09/14-11/10
1996	10/05-12/01	11/02-12/29	09/28-11/24	09/28-11/24	10/31-01/31	09/07-11/03	09/07-11/03	10/26-01/26	09/28-11/24	11/09-02/09	11/30-02/09	01/04-02/09	09/14-11/10
1997	10/04-11/30	11/01-12/28	10/04-11/30	10/04-11/30	10/31-01/31	09/06-11/02	09/06-11/02	10/25-01/25	09/27-11/23	11/08-02/08	11/29-02/08	01/03-02/08	09/13-11/09
1998	10/03-11/29	11/07-01/03	10/03-11/29	09/12-09/20	10/31-01/31	09/05-11/01	09/05-11/01	10/24-01/24	09/26-11/22	11/07-02/07	11/28-02/07	01/02-02/07	09/12-11/08
1999	10/02-11/28	11/06-01/02	10/02-11/28	09/11-09/19	10/30-01/30	09/11-11/07	09/11-11/07	10/30-01/30	09/25-11/21	11/13-02/13	12/04-02/13	01/08-02/13	09/11-11/07
2000	10/07-12/03	11/04-12/31	09/30-11/26	09/09-09/17	10/31-01/31	09/16-11/12	09/16-11/12	11/04-02/04	09/23-11/19	11/11-02/11	12/02-02/11	12/30-02/04	09/09-11/05
2001	10/07-12/03	11/03-12/30	09/29-11/25	09/08-09/16	10/31-01/31	09/15-11/11	09/15-11/11	11/03-02/03	09/22-11/18	11/10-02/10	12/01-02/10	12/29-01/20	09/15-11/11
2002	10/05-12/01	11/02-12/29	09/28-11/24	09/07-09/15	10/31-01/31	09/21-11/17	09/21-10/27	11/09-02/09	09/21-11/17	11/09-02/09	11/30-02/09	12/21-01/19	09/14-11/10
2003	10/04-11/30	11/01-12/28	09/27-11/23	09/06-09/14	10/31-01/31	09/20-11/16	09/20-10/26	10/30-01/30	09/27-11/23	11/01-02/01	11/22-02/01	12/20-01/18	09/13-11/09
2004	10/02-11/28	11/06-01/02	09/25-11/21	09/11-09/19	10/31-01/31	09/18-11/14	09/18-10/24	10/30-01/30	09/25-11/21	11/06-02/01	11/27-02/01	12/18-01/16	09/18-11/14
2005	10/01-11/27	11/09-01/05	09/24-11/20	09/10-09/18	10/31-01/31	09/17-11/13	09/17-10/23	10/29-01/29	09/24-11/20	11/05-02/05	11/26-02/05	12/24-01/29	09/17-11/13

MT[1] Central Flyway portion of MT., except that area south of I-90 and west of the Bighorn River and Sheridan Co

MT[2] Sheridan County, MT

ND[1] Area 1, ND

ND[2] Area 2, ND.

TX[1] Area A, TX

TX[2] Area B, TX

TX[3] Area C, TX

D.E. SHARP

S: CF_D projects CRANES mcp Shcranerep.xls

06/13/06

Table 5. Estimated retrieved harvests of Mid-Continent sandhill cranes in the U.S.

YR	CO	KS	MT	NM	ND	OK	SD	TX	WY	CENTRAL FLYWAY	AZ[4]	NM[4]	AK[2,3]	TOTAL	U.S. TOTAL
1975	91		16	911	2,122	142	86	6,123	6	9,497			1,094	1,094	10,591
1976	106		29	858	52	200	12	6,122	14	7,393			637	637	8,030
1977	39		18	1,456	4,078	410	47	6,094	9	12,151			471	471	12,622
1978	106		36	1,089	2,777	389	19	5,720	10	10,146			239	239	10,385
1979	129		14	1,170	2,733	397	19	5,917	0	10,379			517	517	10,896
1980	68		16	1,019	2,245	363	130	6,305	6	10,152			809	809	10,961
1981	92		11	907	2,395	397	78	6,245	9	10,134	20		383	403	10,537
1982	49		21	335	2,469	535	212	4,295	0	7,916	62		1,160	1,222	9,138
1983	70		28	354	6,471	373	177	5,471	15	12,959	17		1,540	1,557	14,516
1984	85		15	414	4,367	433	139	5,811	7	11,271	23		1,986	2,009	13,280
1985	82		7	334	4,650	416	101	7,184	2	12,776	48		1,197	1,245	14,021
1986	33		1	250	6,563	392	99	5,149	0	12,487	108	184	539	831	13,318
1987	86		15	159	5,334	957	99	6,117	3	12,770	127	318	836	1,281	14,051
1988	68		18	372	3,815	1,061	100	7,330	8	12,772	172	127	1,241	1,540	14,312
1989	25		33	319	4,656	1,003	194	7,400	9	13,639	126	138	545	809	14,448
1990	87		44	377	6,804	698	165	9,865	1	18,041	114	259	918	1,291	19,332
1991	224		31	593	4,580	604	128	6,916	3	13,079	172	235	677	1,084	14,163
1992	84		103	505	4,654	478	141	6,455	13	12,433	139	54	640	833	13,266
1993	112	602	95	506	6,985	826	110	8,769	0	18,005	113	178	201	492	18,497
1994	143	767	56	357	6,235	1,167	239	7,233	4	16,201	86	153	648	887	17,088
1995	208	990	156	673	7,017	1,091	170	10,322	1	20,628	124	111	812	1,047	21,675
1996	91	933	58	332	6,639	1,066	166	7,816	10	17,111	114	78	1,205	1,397	18,508
1997	168	1,167	45	248	6,545	600	189	10,800	4	19,766	171	45	870	1,086	20,852
1998	64	1,362	17	258	7,967	645	454	9,054	10	19,831	114	55	1,042	1,211	21,042
1999	56	1,455	29	321	5,748	879	184	8,469	8	17,149	92	101	NA*	193	17,342
2000	363	590	15	311	5,081	552	374	8,208	10	15,504	166	100	985	1,251	16,755
2001	257	1,033	43	297	5,173	713	478	6,999	7	15,000	154	106	941	1,201	16,201
2002	294	1,067	23	342	2,852	490	160	7,837	22	13,087	197	92	850	1,139	14,226
2003	230	942	49	617	4,564	200	166	11,560	5	18,335	155	162	330	647	18,982
2004	92	856	54	350	3,967	441	67	8,715	4	14,546	192	167	438	797	15,343
2005¹	266	475	67	575	3,792	513	190	12,681	16	18,575	227	175	384	786	19,361

AVERAGES

YR	CO	KS	MT	NM	ND	OK	SD	TX	WY	CENTRAL FLYWAY	AZ[4]	NM[4]	AK[2,3]	TOTAL	U.S. TOTAL
1975-79	94		23	1,097	2,352	308	37	5,995	8	9,913			592	592	10,505
1980-89	66		17	446	4,297	593	133	6,131	6	11,688	78	192	1,024	1,171	12,858
1990-99	124	1,039	63	417	6,317	805	195	8,570	5	17,224	124	127	779	952	18,177
2000-04	247	898	37	383	4,327	479	249	8,664	10	15,294	173	125	709	1,007	16,301
1975-04	120	980	37	534	4,651	597	157	7,343	7	13,839	117	140	819	974	14,813

CURRENT YEAR PERCENT CHANGE FROM:

	CO	KS	MT	NM	ND	OK	SD	TX	WY	CENTRAL FLYWAY	AZ[4]	NM[4]	AK[2,3]	TOTAL	U.S. TOTAL
2004	189%	-45%	24%	64%	-4%	16%	184%	46%	300%	28%	18%	5%	-12%	-1%	26%
1975-79	182%		196%	-48%	61%	67%	419%	112%	105%	87%			-35%	-33%	84%
1980-89	304%		306%	29%	-12%	-13%	43%	107%	171%	59%	191%	-9%	-62%	-33%	51%
1990-99	115%	-54%	6%	38%	-40%	-36%	-2%	48%	196%	8%	83%	38%	-51%	-17%	7%
2000-04	8%	-47%	82%	50%	-12%	7%	-24%	46%	60%	21%	31%	40%	-46%	-22%	19%
1975-04	122%	-52%	83%	8%	-18% #	-14%	21%	73%	138%	34%	94%	25%	-53%	-19%	31%

¹ Preliminary

² A proportion of the Alaskan harvest is composed of lesser sandhill cranes from the Pacific Coast Population

³ Harvest data are from state harvest surveys for only the MCP portion of the state, except in 1977-81, 1986, 1991, and 1998-99 where federal MQS state totals are prorated by the long-term percent MC cranes; data from 2000 forward are MC portion from HIP.

⁴ This MC harvest for AZ and NM represents MC sandhill cranes that were harvested in RMP areas and are not represented in the CF MC Sandhill Crane Federal Harvest Survey

* No estimate is available.

Table 6. Estimated retrieved harvests of Mid-Continent sandhill cranes in Canada.

YEAR	MB	SK	TOTAL
1971	228	2,715	2,943
1972	113	2,030	2,143
1973	683	3,592	4,275
1974	58	6,641	6,699
1975	164	6,000	6,164
1976	210	1,425	1,635
1977	367	N/A	367
1978	876	N/A	876
1979	977	2,821	3,798
1980	892	4,690	5,582
1981	508	2,451	2,959
1982	796	2,041	2,837
1983	378	2,720	3,098
1984	674	3,043	3,717
1985	691	4,468	5,159
1986	1,651	4,455	6,106
1987	795	4,472	5,267
1988	1,955	4,991	6,946
1989	2,666	2,318	4,984
1990	1,018	3,821	4,839
1991	1,800	3,594	5,394
1992	1,205	4,440	5,645
1993	482	2,309	2,791
1994	529	3,259	3,788
1995	1,005	4,824	5,829
1996	1,352	2,961	4,313
1997	1,279	4,622	5,901
1998	889	8,636	9,525
1999	1,300	7,100	8,400
2000	805	8,645	9,450
2001	1,247	7,538	8,785
2002	1,283	6,665	7,948
2003	1,474	8,112	9,586
2004	1,267	9,769	11,036
2005	1,776	8,101	9,877

AVERAGES:			
1971-79	408	3,603	3,211
1980-89	1,101	3,565	4,666
1990-99	1,086	4,557	5,643
2000-04	1,215	8,146	9,361
1971-04	930	4,599	5,258

CURRENT YEAR PERCENT CHANGE FROM:			
2004	40%	-17%	-11%
1971-79	335%	125%	208%
1980-89	61%	127%	112%
1990-99	64%	78%	75%
2000-04	46%	-1%	6%
1971-04	91%	76%	88%

Table 7. Annual sport hunting mortality estimates for the Mid-Continent Population of sandhill cranes in North America.

YR	SPORT HUNTING MORTALITY					
	Retrieved				Unretrieved	Total
	Central Flyway	Other Survey Total	Canada	Mexico[2]	No. Am.[3]	
1975	9,497	1,094	6,164	1,676	3,672	22,102
1976	7,393	637	1,635	967	2,032	12,663
1977	12,151	471	367	1,299	2,440	16,728
1978	10,146	239	876	1,126	2,308	14,695
1979	10,379	517	3,798	1,469	2,807	18,970
1980	10,152	809	5,582	1,654	3,349	21,546
1981	10,134	403	2,959	1,350	2,722	17,568
1982	7,916	1,222	2,837	1,198	2,451	15,624
1983	12,959	1,557	3,098	1,761	3,503	22,879
1984	11,271	2,009	3,717	1,700	3,375	22,072
1985	12,776	1,245	5,159	1,918	3,524	24,622
1986	12,487	831	6,106	1,942	3,646	25,012
1987	12,770	1,281	5,267	1,932	3,406	24,656
1988	12,772	1,540	6,946	2,126	3,750	27,134
1989	13,639	809	4,984	1,943	3,628	25,003
1990	18,041	1,291	4,839	2,417	4,228	30,817
1991	13,079	1,084	5,394	1,956	3,455	24,967
1992	12,433	833	5,645	1,891	3,133	23,935
1993	18,005	492	2,791	2,129	3,334	26,751
1994	16,201	887	3,788	2,088	3,029	25,992
1995	20,628	1,047	5,829	2,750	4,161	34,416
1996	17,111	1,397	4,313	2,282	3,609	28,713
1997	19,766	1,086	5,901	2,675	4,211	33,640
1998	19,831	1,211	9,525	3,057	4,901	38,524
1999	17,149	193*	8,400	2,574	3,950	32,267
2000	15,504	1,251	9,450	2,621	4,093	32,919
2001	15,000	1,201	8,785	2,499	4,014	31,499
2002	13,087	1,139	7,948	2,217	3,448	27,839
2003	18,335	647	9,586	2,857	4,246	35,671
2004[1]	14,546	797	11,036	2,638	4,165	33,182
2005[1]	18,575	786	9,877	2,924	4,512	36,674
AVERAGES:						
1975-79	9,913	592	2,568	1,307	2,652	17,032
1980-89	11,688	1,171	4,666	1,752	3,336	22,612
1990-99	17,224	1,036	5,643	2,382	3,801	30,002
2000-04	15,294	1,007	9,361	2,566	3,993	32,222
1975-04	13,839	1,001	5,424	2,024	3,486	25,747
CURRENT YEAR PERCENT CHANGE FROM:						
2004	28%	-1%	-11%	11%	8%	11%
1975-79	87%	33%	285%	124%	70%	115%
1980-89	59%	-33%	112%	67%	35%	62%
1990-99	8%	-24%	75%	23%	19%	22%
2000-04	21%	-22%	6%	14%	13%	14%
1975-04	34%	-21%	82%	44%	29%	42%

[1] Preliminary   *D.E. SHARP S:\CF_D\projects\CRANES\mcp\Shcranerep.xls*   *06/13/06*

[2] Unknown harvests (Mexico) were assumed to be 10% of harvests in the U.S. and Canada.

[3] Unretrieved kill as reported by hunters is used for the Central Flyway; for the remainder of harvest areas, it is assumed to be 20% of retrieved harvests.

*There is no estimate available for AK in that year.

Table 8. Estimated retrieved harvests of the Rocky Mountain Population of greater sandhill cranes.

YR	UT	NM	AZ	WY	MT	ID	TOTAL
1981			20				20
1982			9	143			152
1983			35	154			189
1984			33	101			134
1985			40	138			178
1986			23	195			218
1987			60	190			250
1988		310	40	128			478
1989	54	483	51	125			713
1990	35	79	9	58			181
1991	48	47	44	101			240
1992		147	39	168	42		396
1993	28	297	61	115	45		546
1994	34	416	27	150	40		667
1995	27	270	33	77	41		448
1996	32	236	27	84	49	20	448
1997	30	114	22	82	62	136	446
1998	34	180	37	93	59	135	538
1999	54	198	21	124	71	190	658 [1]
2000	69	257	37	163	91	193	810 [2]
2001	77	288	26	142	87	278	898
2002	60	160	42	132	51	194	639
2003	57	169	34	72	50	146	528
2004	53	189	35	124	51	142	594
2005	62	236	50	116	49	189	702

AVERAGES:							
1981-89	54	397	35	147			259
1990-99	36	198	32	105	51	120	457
2000-04	63	213	35	127	66	191	694
1981-04	46	226	34	124	57	159	432

CURRENT YEAR PERCENT CHANGE FROM:							
2004	17%	25%	43%	-6%	-4%	33%	18%
1981-89	15%	-40%	45%	-21%			171%
1990-99	73%	19%	56%	10%	-4%	57%	54%
2000-04	-2%	11%	44%	-8%	-26%	-1%	1%
1981-04	34%	4%	49%	-7%	-14%	19%	62%

[1] RMP Sandill cranes (40) were also taken as part of research project in the San Luis Valley, CO   *D.E. SHARP*   *S:CF D projects CRANES mcp Shcranerep.xls   06 13 06*

[2] RMP Sandill cranes (20) were also taken as part of research project in the San Luis Valley, CO

Table 9. Spring population indices for Rocky Mountain sandhill cranes, 1984 - 96.

| YR | SAN LUIS VALLEY, COLORADO | | | | | SURVEY COND. |
	RAW COUNT	ADJ. FOR EST. BIAS[1]	ADJ. TO REM. LES.[2]	OTHER AREAS	INDEX	
1984	10,962	14,488	13,562	550	14,112	POOR
1985	18,393	21,773	20,382	0	20,382	GOOD
1986	14,031	14,031	13,135	20	13,155	POOR
1987	13,561	15,661	14,660	0	14,660	POOR
1988	17,510	17,510	16,381	22	16,403	POOR
1989	17,302	18,389	17,004	0	17,004	GOOD
1990	20,851	24,593	21,221	275	21,496	GOOD
1991	19,990	18,405	16,045	175	16,220	GOOD
1992	23,516	23,516	19,999	9	20,008	GROUND
1993	17,576	17,576	16,478	1,260	17,738	POOR
1994	17,229	16,036	15,063	203	15,266	FAIR
1995	25,276	23,390	20,229	0	20,229	GOOD
1996	23,019	26,379	22,737	1,010	23,747	GOOD

[1] Raw estimate adjusted by photography for estimation bias
[2] Population estimate adjusted to remove the number of lesser sandhill cranes (non-RMP cranes).

Table 10. Fall pre-migration population indices for Rocky Mountain sandhill cranes.

YR	UT	CO	ID	WY	MT	TOTAL	3-YR AVG
1987	1,578	1,443	10,686	2,327	1,447	17,481	
1992	2,810	3,181	5,801	2,241	5,264	19,297	
1995	1,528	2,284	6,864	1,671	3,681	16,028	
1996	1,849	1,255	8,334	2,526	2,974	16,938	
1997[1,2]	2,450	1,604	8,132	2,255	3,595	18,036	17,001
1998	2,185	1,273	8,067	3,262	3,415	18,202	17,725
1999	2,292	1,102	8,761	4,205	3,141	19,501	18,580
2000	2,416	749	9,337	3,890	3,598	19,990	19,231
2001	1,522	666	7,160	2,626	4,585	16,559	18,683
2002	1,869	1,355	7,698	3,038	4,843	18,803	18,451
2003	2,546	745	7,822	3,446	4,964	19,523	18,295
2004	2,239	1,410	7,152	3,072	4,637	18,510	18,945
2005	2,646	1,052	7,668	3,911	5,588	20,865	19,633

[1] Incomplete survey efforts in years prior might have resulted in lower estimates; the official count begins in 1997.

[2] In October 1997, a special survey was also conducted in the SLV, Colorado and other areas, which resulted in a total

of 27,090 Rocky Mountain and Mid-Continent cranes being counted.

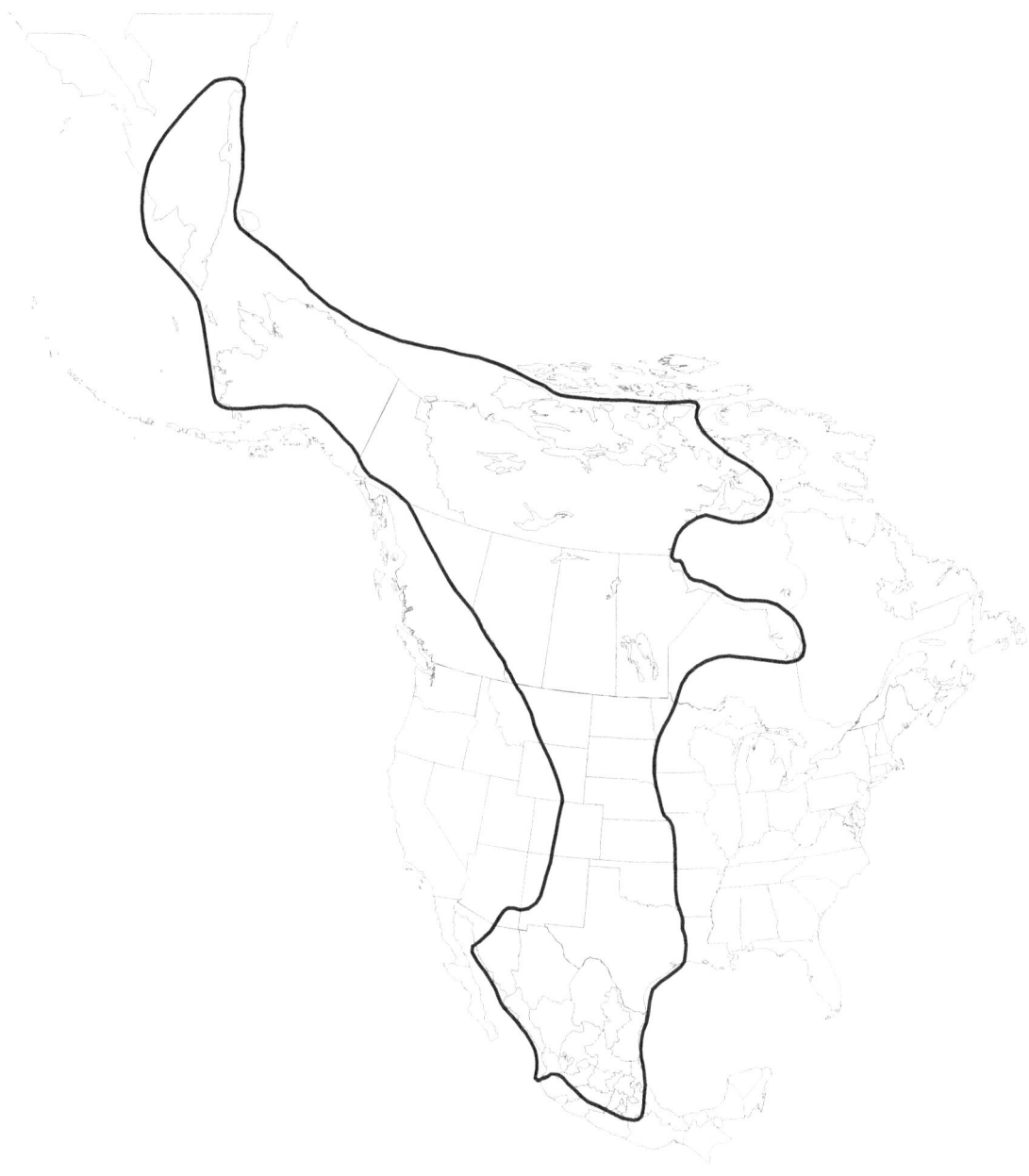

Fig. 1. Approximate range of Mid-Continent sandhill cranes (based on figures in Sharp et al. 2000, Tacha et al. 1994, and data from radio-telemetered birds provided by G. Krapu, Northern Prairie Wildlife Research Center, Jamestown, ND).

Breeding Range

Primary Staging Area

Wintering Range

---------- Pacific/Central Flyway Boundary

Figure 2. Approximate range of the Rocky Mountain Population of Greater Sandhill
Cranes.

Figure 3. Areas open to the hunting of Mid-Continent sandhill cranes by Federal frameworks in the Central Flyway states, 2004-05.

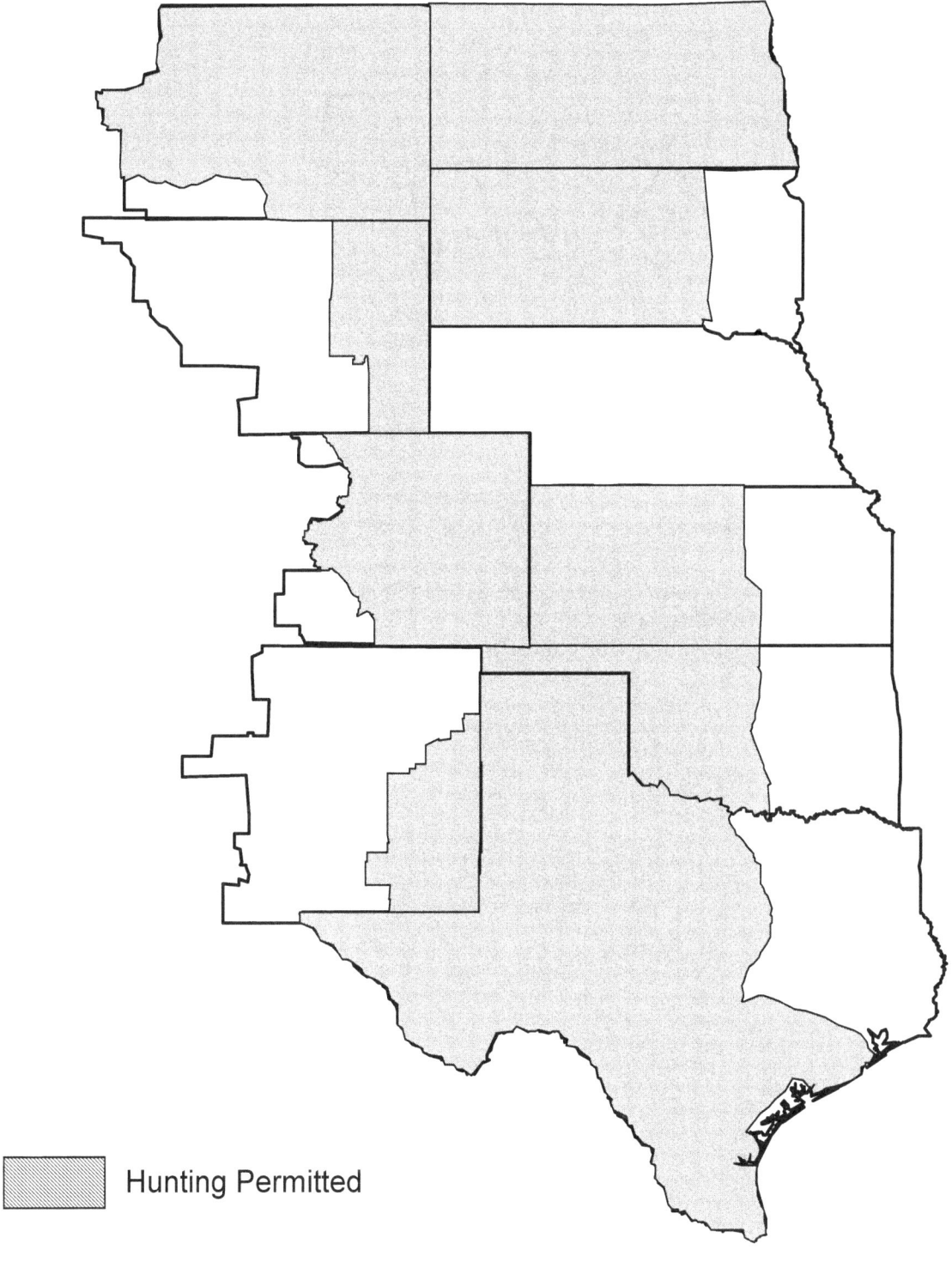

Hunting Permitted

Figure 4. Spring population indices for Mid-Continent sandhill cranes on the Central Platte River Valley, Nebraska.

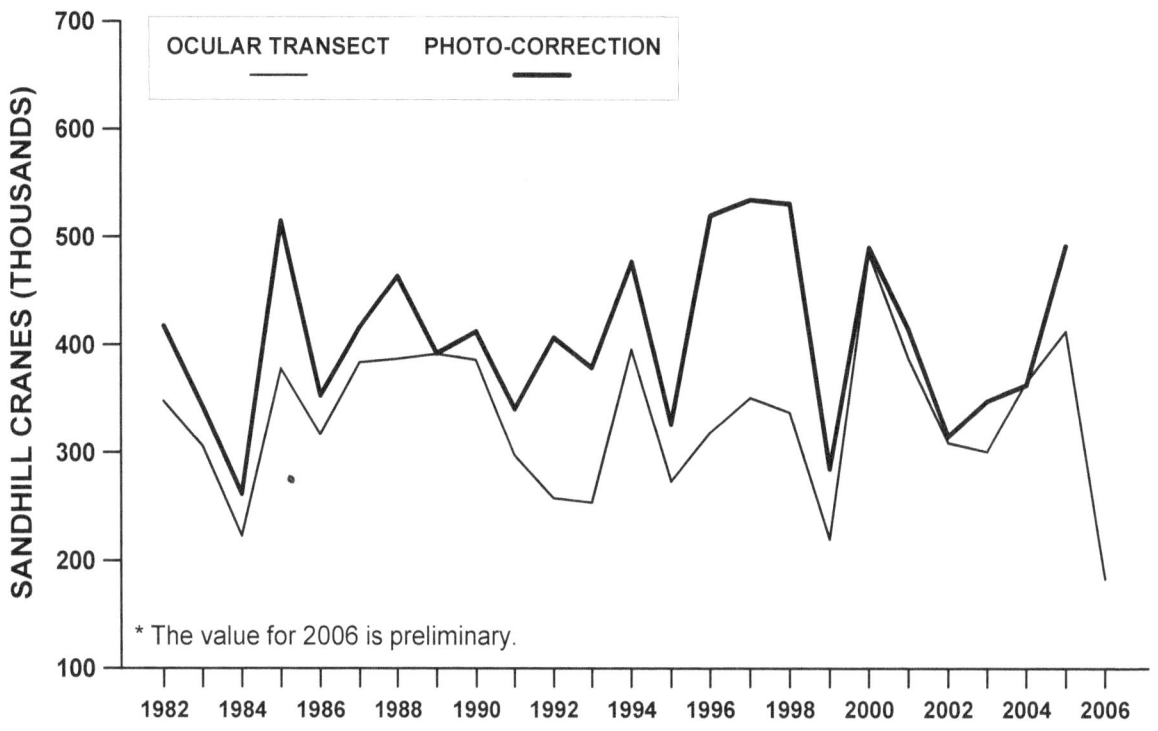

Figure 5. Photo-corrected spring population estimates (solid line) and the 95% confidence intervals (dashed lines) for Mid-Continent sandhill cranes on the Central Platte River Valley, Nebraska.

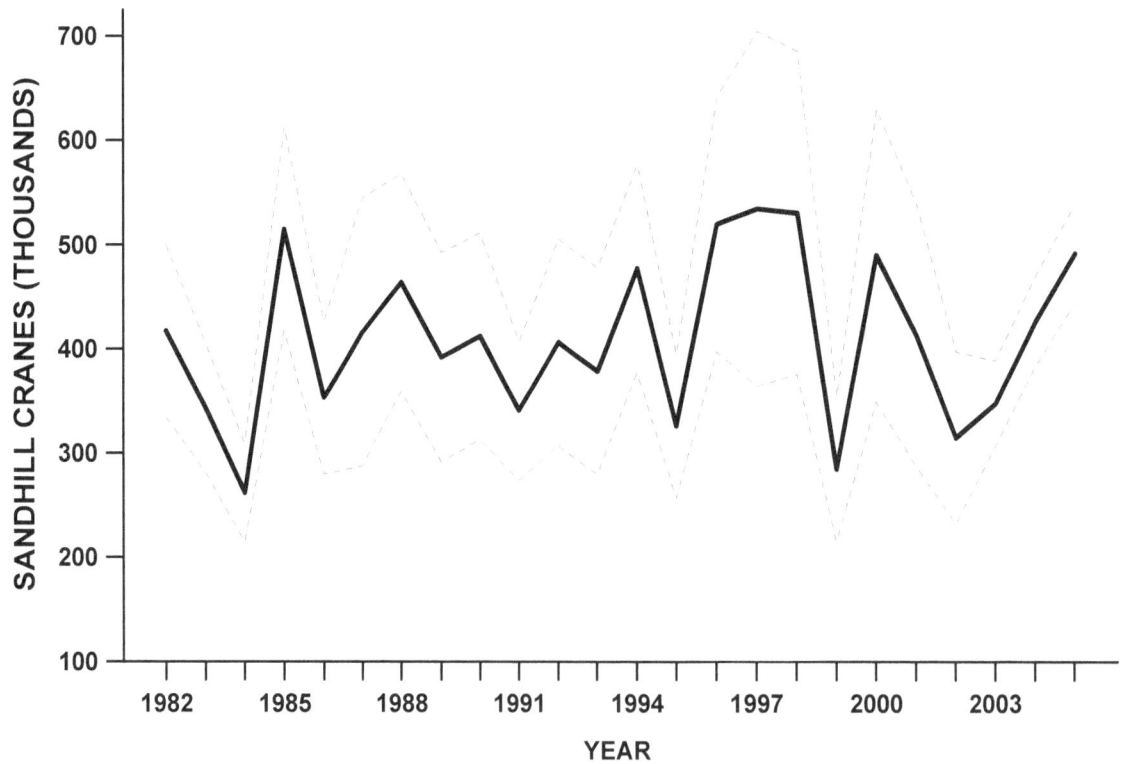

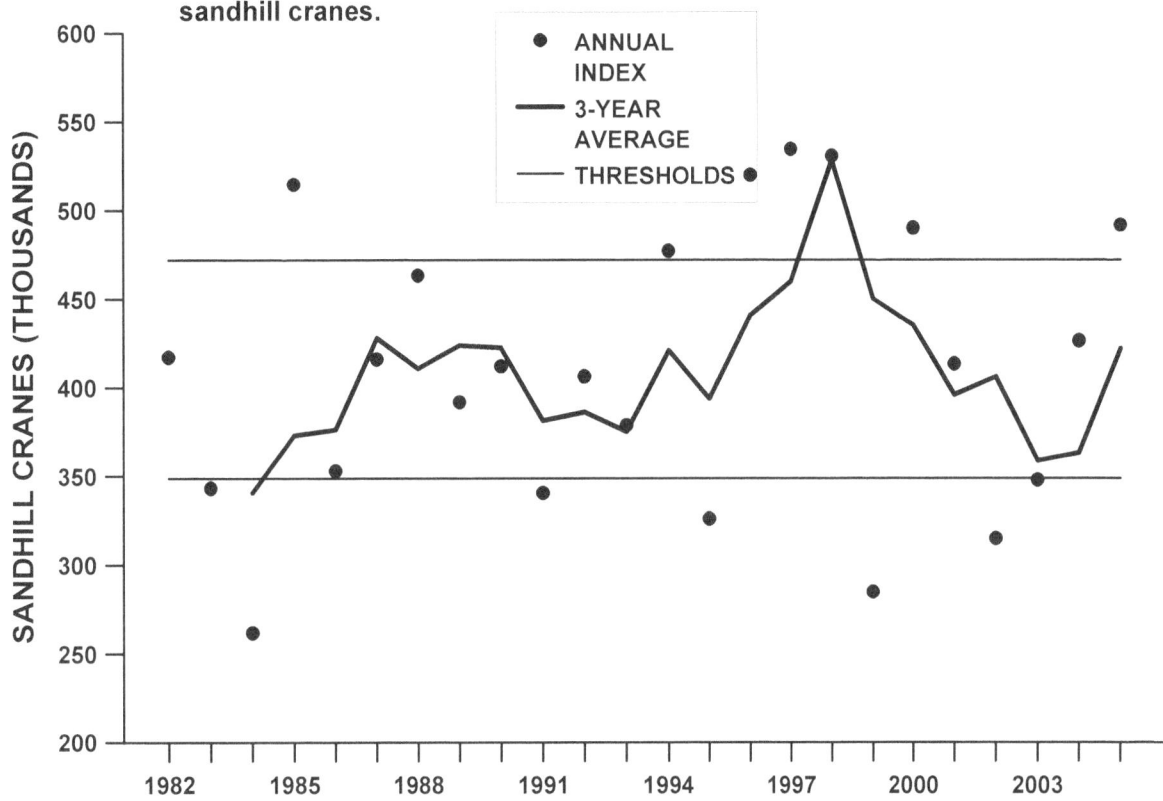

Figure 6. Annual and three-year average photo-corrected ocular transect spring population indices and population objective thresholds for Mid-Continent sandhill cranes.

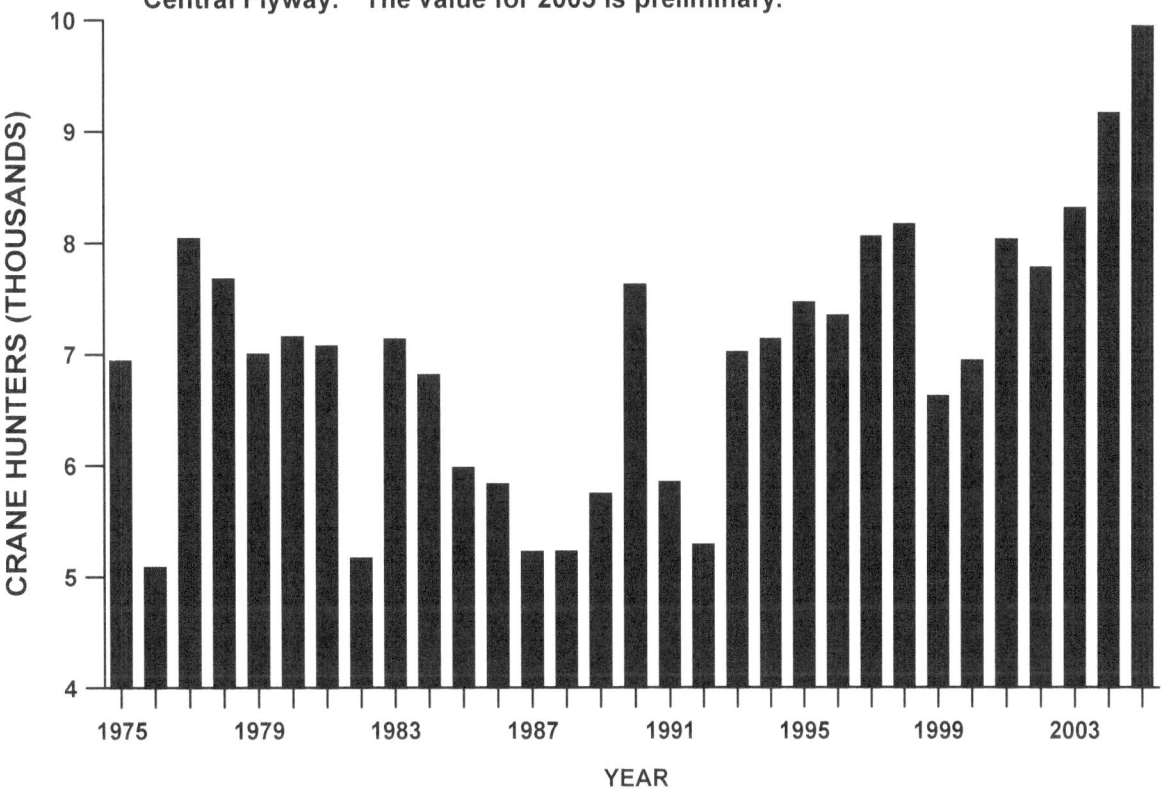

Figure 7. Active Mid-Continent sandhill crane hunters in the U.S. portion of the Central Flyway. * The value for 2005 is preliminary.

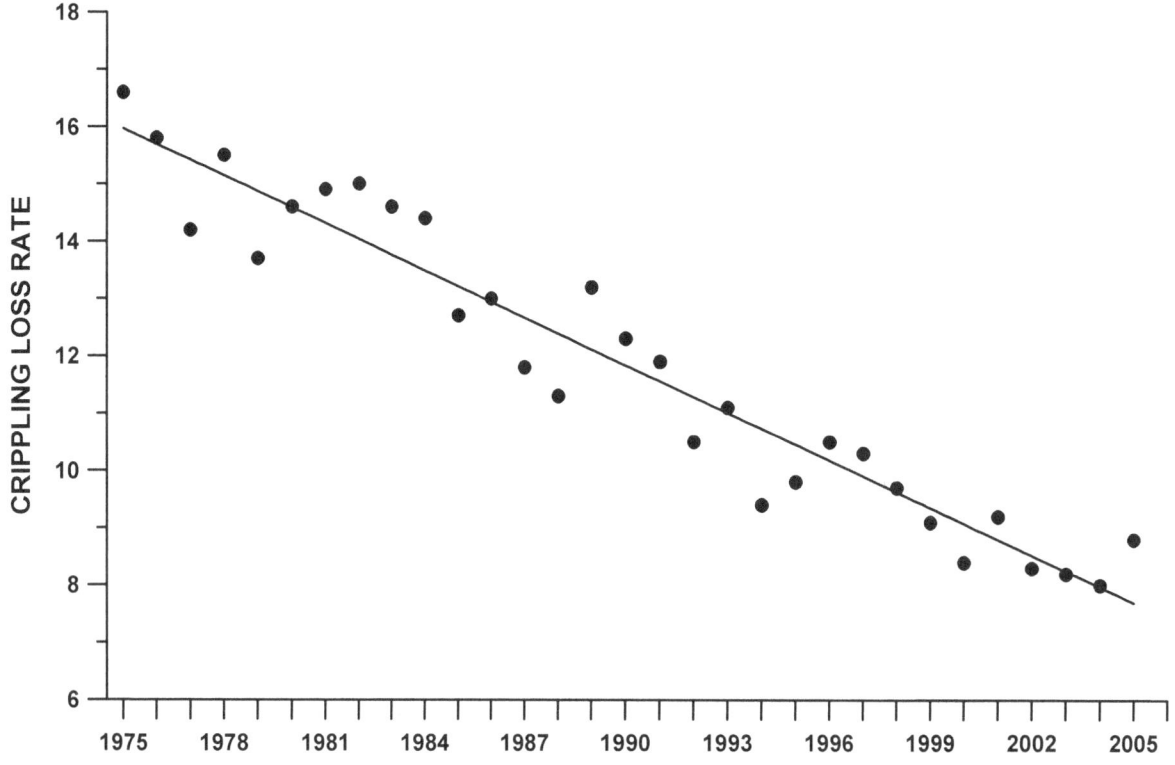

Figure 8. Crippling loss rate (number lost/[number retrieved + lost]) of Mid-Continent sandhill cranes in the U.S. portion of the Central Flyway.

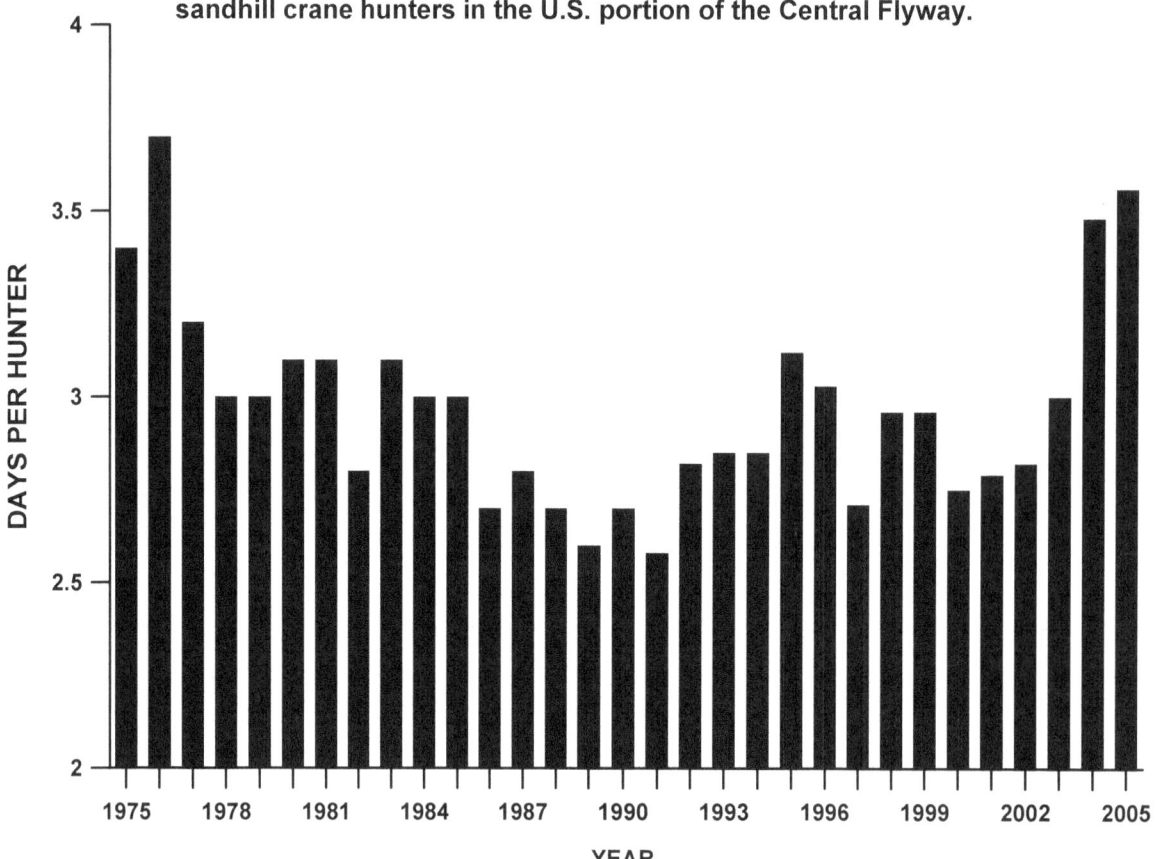

Figure 9. Average number of hunting days afield reported by active Mid-Continent sandhill crane hunters in the U.S. portion of the Central Flyway.

YEAR

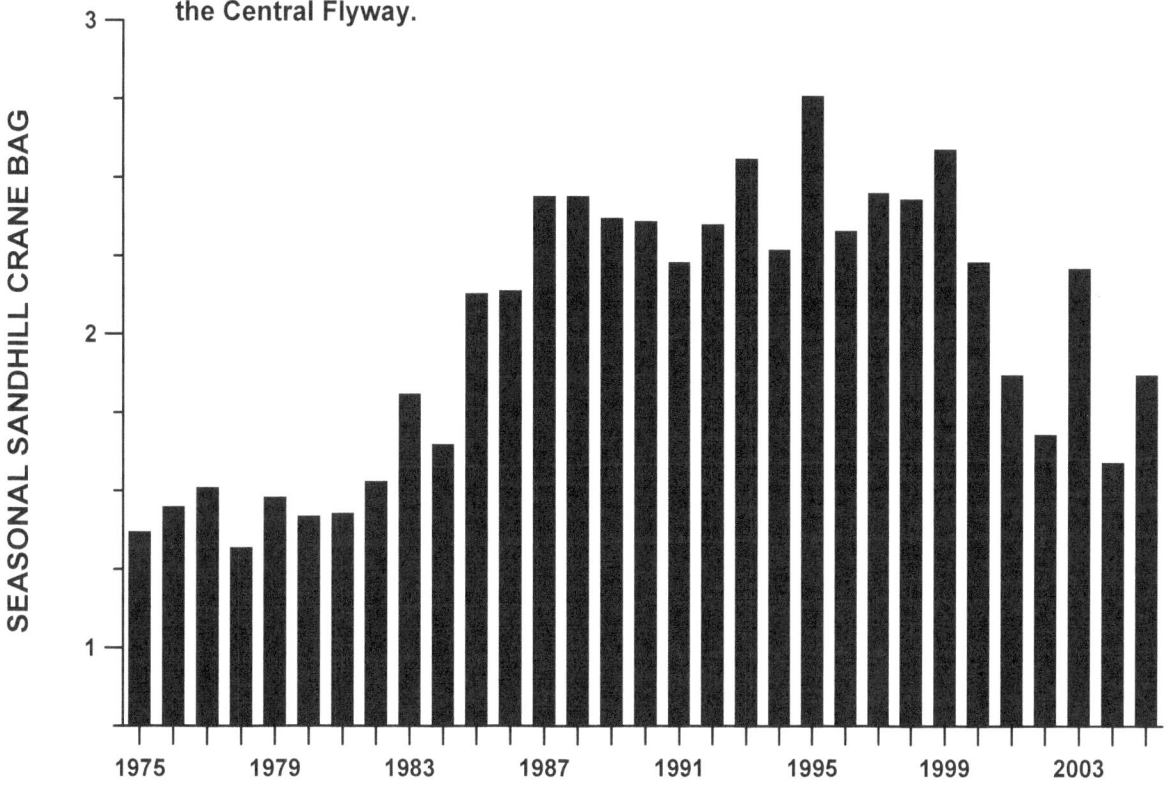

Figure 10. Seasonal bag per Mid-Continent sandhill crane hunter in the U.S. portion of the Central Flyway.

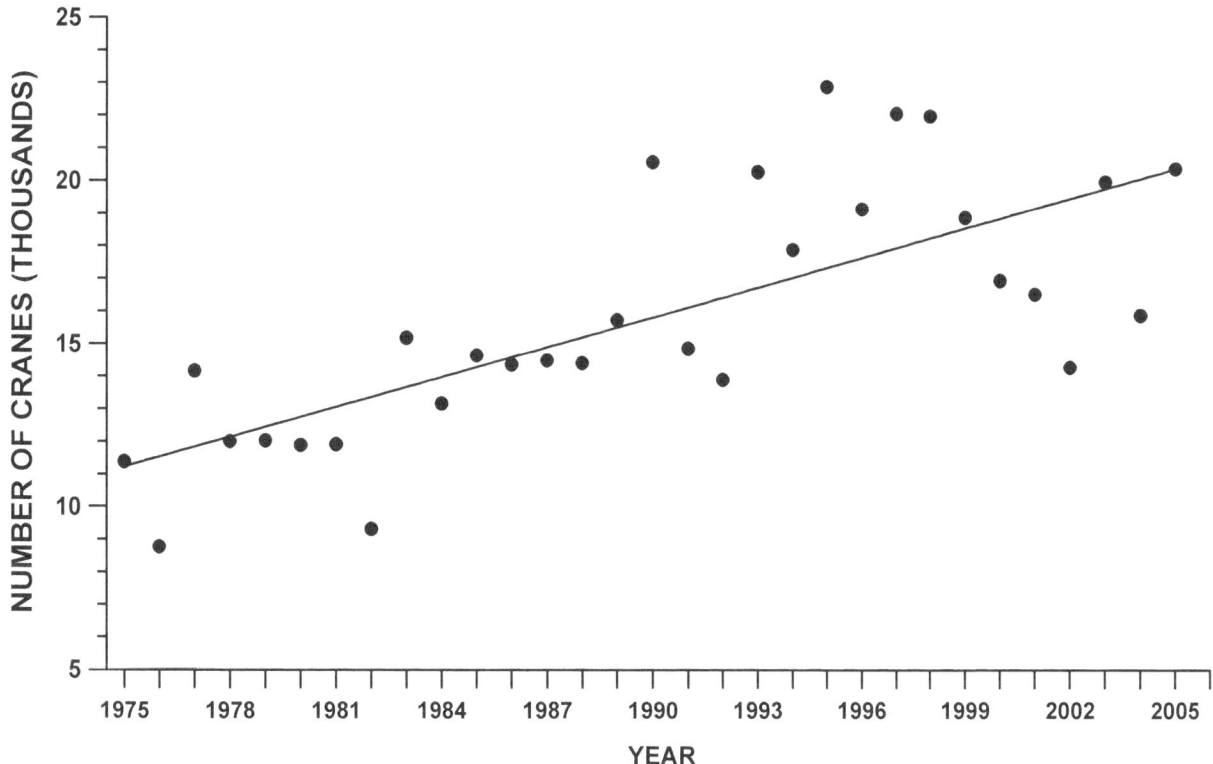

Figure 11. Estimated hunting mortality (retrieved and unretrieved) of Mid-Continent sandhill cranes in the U.S. portion of the Central Flyway.

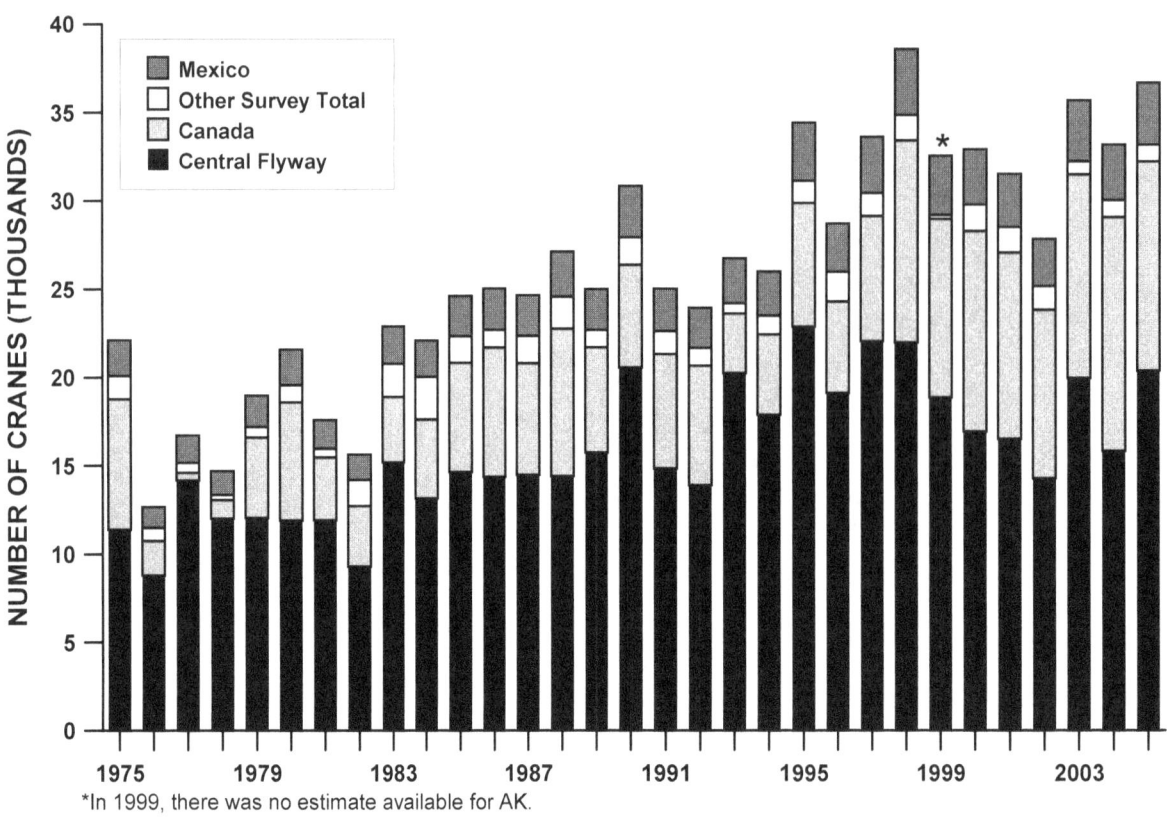

Figure 12. Estimated hunting mortality (retrieved and unretrieved) of Mid-Continent sandhill cranes in North America.

*In 1999, there was no estimate available for AK.

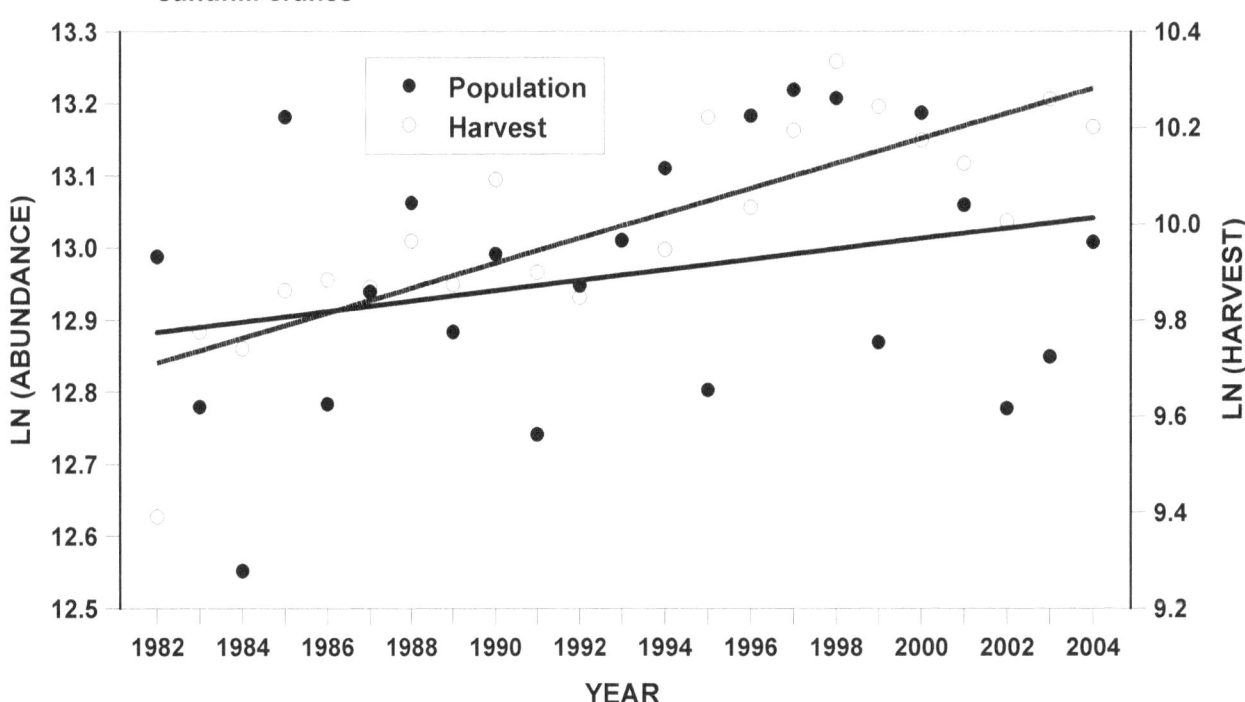

Figure 13. Trend analyses of indices to abundance and harvest of Mid-Continent sandhill cranes

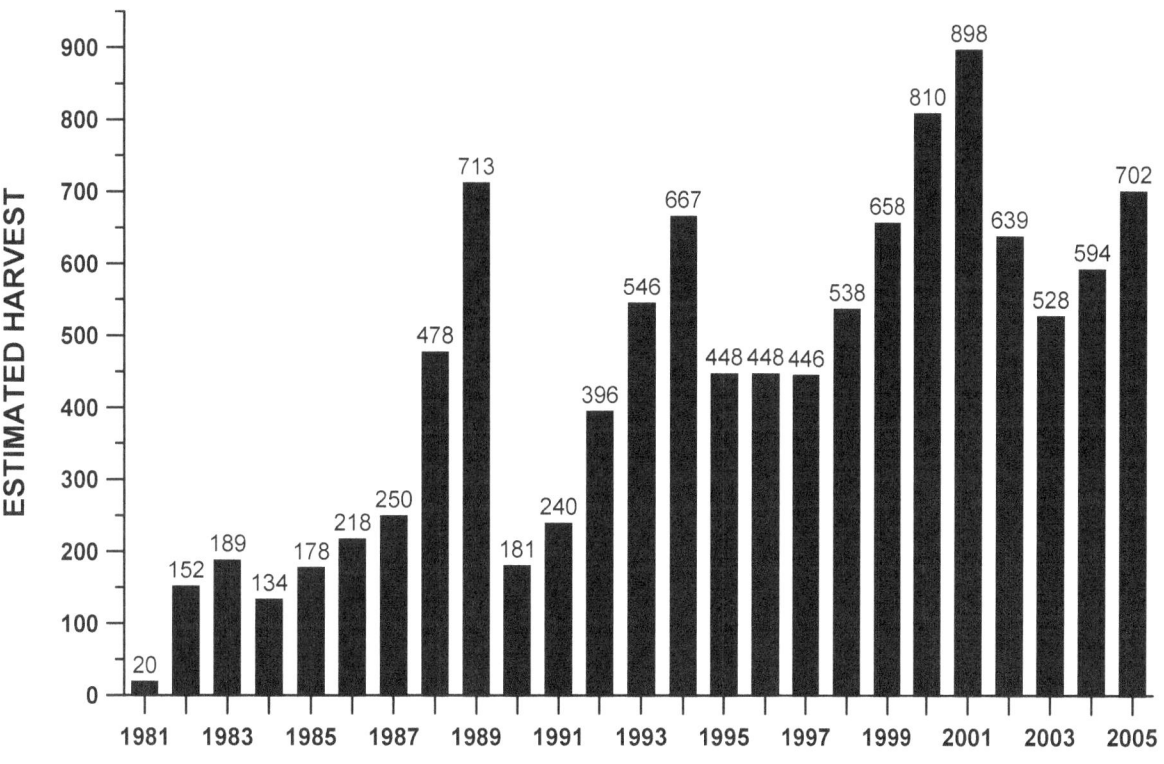

Figure 14. Estimated harvest of Rocky Mountain Population sandhill cranes.

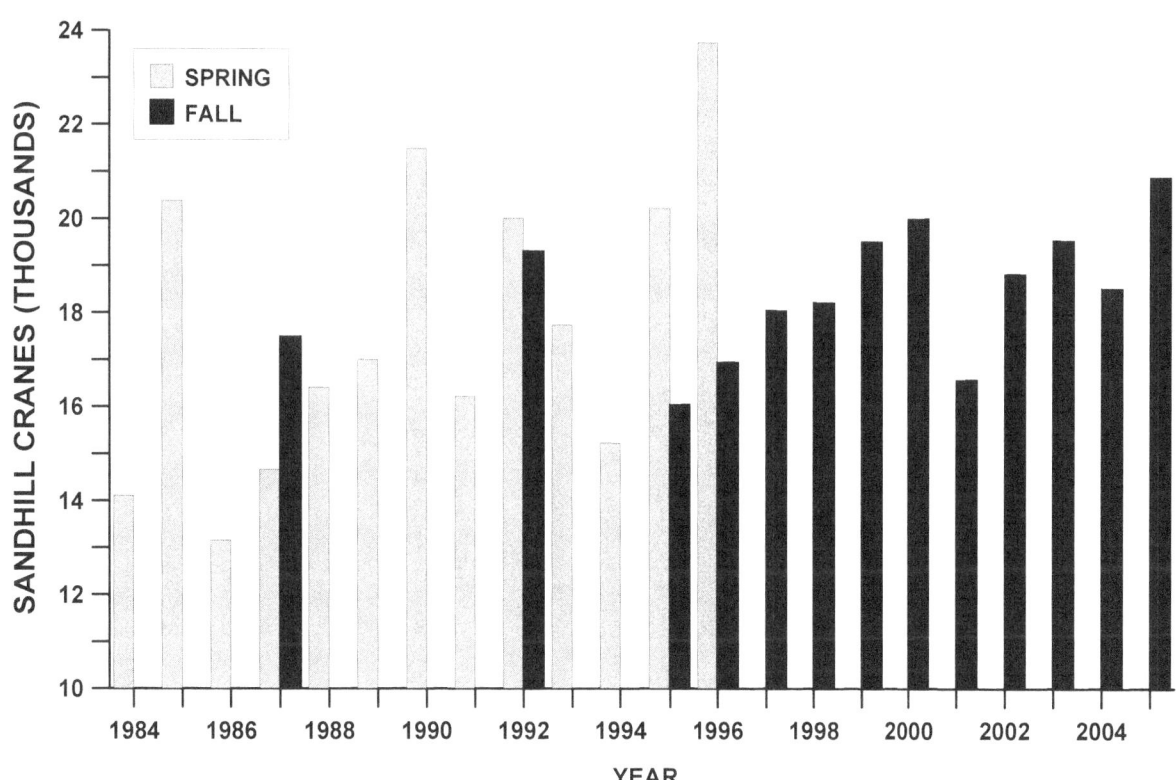

Figure 15. Abundance indices for the Rocky Mountain Population of sandhill cranes
(Incomplete survey efforts in years prior to 1997 might have resulted in lower estimates;
the official count begins in 1997

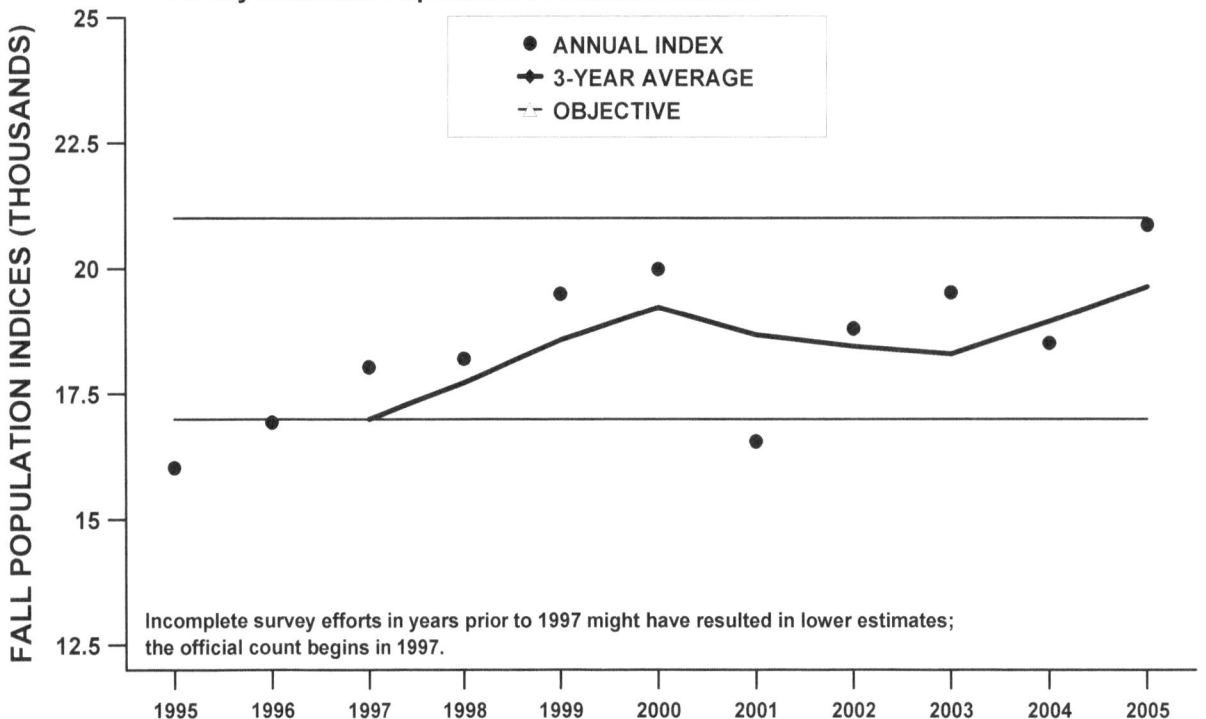

Figure 16. Annual and three-year average of fall pre-migration abundance indices for the Rocky Mountain Population of sandhill cranes.

Incomplete survey efforts in years prior to 1997 might have resulted in lower estimates; the official count begins in 1997.

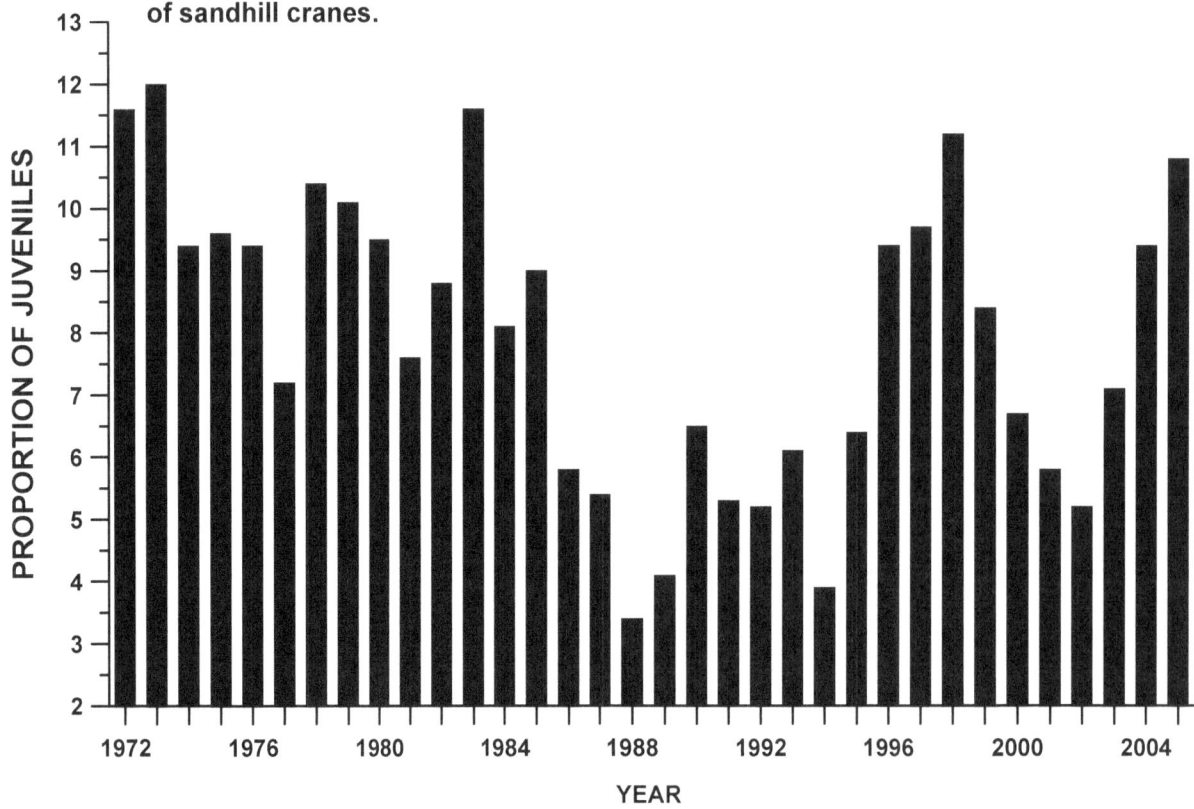

Figure 17. Annual indices for recruitment (% juveniles) of the Rocky Mountain Population of sandhill cranes.

www.ingramcontent.com/pod-product-compliance
Lightning Source LLC
Chambersburg PA
CBHW082203290526

45794CB00008B/3411